Letters to New Pastors

Letters to New Pastors

Michael Jinkins

William B. Eerdmans Publishing Company

Grand Rapids, Michigan / Cambridge, U.K.

© 2006 Wm. B. Eerdmans Publishing Co.

Wm. B. Eerdmans Publishing Co.
255 Jefferson Ave. S.E., Grand Rapids, Michigan 49503 /
P.O. Box 163, Cambridge CB3 9PU U.K.
www.eerdmans.com

Printed in the United States of America

10 09 08 07 06   7 6 5 4 3 2 1

Library of Congress Cataloging-in-Publication Data

Jinkins, Michael, 1953-
Letters to new pastors / Michael Jinkins.
p.   cm.
Includes bibliographical references (p.   ).
ISBN-10: 0-8028-2751-9 / ISBN-13: 978-0-8028-2751-7 (pbk.: alk. paper)
1. Clergy — Office.   2. Clergy — Appointment, call, and election.   I. Title.

BV660.3.J56 2006
253 — dc22

2005032912

Excerpt from "Kitty Hawk" from THE POETRY OF ROBERT FROST edited by
Edward Connery Lathem. Copyright 1969 by Henry Holt and Company.
Copyright 1956, 1962 by Robert Frost. Reprinted by permission of Henry Holt
and Company, LLC.

For *Scott Black Johnston*

"Nothing great comes into being suddenly."

(Epictetus, *Discourses,* Book I)

Contents

Acknowledgments

I want to thank Jon Pott and Reinder VanTil of William B. Eerdmans Publishing Company for their encouragement, and Jon in particular for his invitation to write this book. I am profoundly grateful to the pastors and students who have shared their stories, questions, insights, and reflections with me as I prepared for and wrote this book. I am also grateful to the students of Austin Seminary who are members of my weekly prayer group, Foedus Pietas, who agreed to read and offer critical responses to the letters as I wrote them. These letters bear the indelible stamp of this group's prayerful thought. As always, I am deeply grateful to my colleagues on the faculty of Austin Presbyterian Theological Seminary for their friendship and for their love of the church and Christian ministry, and to President Ted Wardlaw and the Board of Trustees for their unfailing support and encouragement.

This book is gratefully dedicated to my friend Scott Black Johnston, Senior Pastor of Trinity Presbyterian Church, Atlanta, Georgia.

Introduction

Letter writing has almost been eclipsed by the advent of recent communications technologies. I continue to believe in the power of letters, however. I save correspondence from students, colleagues, family, and friends, and read the letters again and again. In the midst of a culture addicted to the ephemeral and the superficial, letters continue to hold the power to make a deep and lasting impression on the recipient. I do not think an e-mail or a phone call from Saint Paul would have had quite the same influence on the early Christians in Rome as did the letter he sent them, which they shared with other churches and passed on to us.

The Christian faith maintains a long and honored tradition of letters written by experienced pastors to their newer colleagues in ministry. Generally speaking, these writings are intended for encouragement and instruction, though sometimes they tend toward admonition and exhortation.

First and Second Timothy stand at the beginning of this tradition. The veteran pastor tells young Timothy to vary his conversation for different members of the congregation — young and old, male and female. He tells Timothy which aspects of his ministry are essential and which are not. He tells him to watch his health ("Take a little wine for the sake of your stomach,"

1 Tim. 5:23); not to be defensive about his age nor allow himself to be discounted because of it either ("Let no one despise your youth," 1 Tim. 4:12); and to hold fast in all things to the faith of the Lord Jesus Christ ("You then, my child, be strong in the grace that is in Christ Jesus," 2 Tim. 2:1). So began the rich tradition of letters to new pastors.

Other letters and books, whether written specifically for the instruction of new pastors or not, have been used by the church for this purpose. Gregory of Nazianzus, writing in the tumultuous fourth century, explains to his congregation why, immediately following his ordination, he literally ran for the hills to escape his vocation and his congregation. In his apologia Gregory presents the first and still the most beautiful and compelling description of the pastoral office. In many ways John Chrysostom's *On the Priesthood* and Gregory the Great's *Pastoral Discipline,* both timeless classics from the ancient church, merely elaborate on the themes laid down by Gregory of Nazianzus. Gregory's friend, Basil of Caesarea (also called Basil the Great), another of the fourth century's heroes of orthodoxy, embeds many of his most important theological insights in letters to priests, old and young. His letters in the Loeb Classics series fill four volumes with pastoral and spiritual wisdom. More familiar to Protestant readers, of course, are George Herbert, *The Country Parson;* Richard Baxter, *The Reformed Pastor;* Charles Haddon Spurgeon, *Lectures to My Students;* Reinhold Niebuhr's diary, published as *Leaves from the Notebook of a Tamed Cynic;* Dietrich Bonhoeffer's *Life Together;* and more recently, the theologically rich reflections of Eugene Peterson and William Willimon, and the memoirs of Richard Lischer.

I never cease to be amazed at how new pastors resonate to the struggles and insights of a reluctant bishop (Gregory) from a nearly forgotten village in Asia Minor, or of an aristocratic poet and rector (Herbert) in seventeenth-century England, or of a young minister (Niebuhr) in Henry Ford's Detroit. Thousands of miles and scores of centuries may separate us from the trials of these pastors and the congregations they served, but we have this calling in common.[1]

I have drawn from this tradition for over thirty years, first as a pastor thirsty to learn from more experienced pastors, and later as a teacher and a colleague of new pastors. The aggregate wisdom of the church benefits new pastors far more than my own idiosyncratic observations could hope to. Thus these letters consciously and deliberately retrieve the classical resources on pastoral ministry for a contemporary audience.

As I began this book, I wanted to connect readers with this deeper, fuller tradition, and to give voice to those men and women who have taught me what it means to be a pastor. I particularly wanted to avoid the conceit of posing as an expert, a posture that can so easily infect this kind of book, giving the arrogant and altogether false impression that the author is a font of wisdom.

When Jon Pott, the editor in chief of Eerdmans, first suggested that I write this book, he recommended that it be a pastoral version of Richard Selzer's *Letters to a Young Doctor*. Although I had originally rejected the epistolary form itself (simply thinking of the title, *Letters to New Pastors,* as a convenient way to introduce the various topics of the pastoral arts in conventional chapters), as this project took shape I realized that a book of letters would be truer to the life of a pastor as I have known it than a straight prosaic treatment. It might also be more interesting to readers. Letters have a way of reflecting the apparent randomness of the pastor's life. They also convey something of the way pastoral wisdom is actually acquired in ministry — unsystematically and episodically. Letters wander peripatetically, looping back on themselves. More than the regurgitation of facts, they reveal something of the soul of the author, and the inner spirit of the subject. Collections of letters sometimes emphasize what is important by repetition, and I have tried to mimic this. There's an almost guilty pleasure in reading collections of letters, a voyeuristic pleasure, in part, but something deeper too. When I read Flannery O'Connor's published collection of letters, *The Habit of Being,* for example, I sense that I am encountering more than her ideas and her thoughts. I sense I am encountering her, in her light moods and her dark ones. And this encounter instructs me personally.[2]

Letters draw us into a living conversation; though, as you will see in this collection, you always tend to be walking in on a conversation that is already in progress, and you are unable to hear (at least directly) the voice of one of the conversation partners in each exchange. I have left a good deal to the imagination of the reader, in part simply out of respect for the reality I am trying to imitate, and in part because I trust the imagination of the reader to fill in the blanks.

Many who have read C. S. Lewis's *Letters to Malcolm: Chiefly on Prayer* agree that one of the things that makes his book spring to life is the way the letters invite us to reflect personally on our own prayer lives, whereas a typical book on the subject of prayer can keep the reader at arm's length. A book of letters is, perhaps, most effective because of its indirect approach to instruction. The reader is invited to consider the advice one correspondent gives another, while not being addressed directly. The reader holds on to his or her freedom, is able to ponder at will the advice, agree or disagree at a distance, be charmed or angered by the author of the letters, while reading intimate documents.

This allows the reader the freedom to try on the reflections of the author to see what fits.

The letters in this book are not written to a single new pastor. There are several recipients of these letters. Malcolm is a young man in his late twenties who went directly from college to seminary to a solo pastorate. Susan is a thirty-something associate pastor who came to ministry from a brief career in advertising. Jim is a recent seminary graduate of more mature years who came to ministry after many years in the corporate world. Dorothy is a second-career pastor struggling to understand the idioms of ministry in a therapeutic age. And there are others. The recipients of these letters are fictional. They are drawn from life. However, though they are based on real pastors, many of them former students I have had the privilege to know for many years, they are composite portraits. No single person was the model for any individual pastor in the book. Their stories, questions, worries, and insights, fresh from letters, e-mails, and phone conversations, are woven and interwoven throughout.

The epistolary form also liberates me as author from the Wizard of Oz–like fiction of hiding in the margins as the omniscient narrator. Strange as it may sound, while I am the author of the book, I am not the author of the letters themselves. The author of the letters is a better and more experienced pastor than I. His voice represents a combination of several voices of pastors, church leaders, and educators I have long admired, respected, and learned from throughout my ministry as a pastor and teacher. There is something of Carlyle Marney, C. Ellis Nelson, James B. Torrance, Bill Fogleman, David Pittenger, Kenneth Bradshaw, Ilene Dunn, Louis Adams, Gordon Edwards, Laura Mendenhall, Ted Wardlaw, Bill Enright, the late Thomas Allsop, and many others, in the voice of the author of these letters. The pastors of my childhood and those I have known as colleagues and friends merge in the authorial voice. The author of the letters also, however, has his own pet peeves and idiosyncrasies and blind spots. There are times when he is charming, devotional, and deeply sensitive. At other times he rants and raves, and even gets angry. My goal has been to make him as real as possible so that we can learn as much from his mistakes, and the way he handles those mistakes, as we do from his pastoral wisdom.

An important source of the questions and issues addressed in these letters was the interaction among students in seminary classes I have taught for many years at Austin Presbyterian Theological Seminary, such as "Entry into Ministry," "The Call to Ministry," "Power and Change in Pastoral Ministry," and "The Future of the Church." These courses have been enriched by the involvement of pastors and other church leaders who have brought their practice of ministry directly into the seminary classroom. Former students of "Entry into Ministry" will, for example, hear echoes in these pages from the pastors who participated in our annual "I wish I'd known then what I know now" seminar panels. Although the anecdotes have been heavily disguised to protect the identities of pastors and church members, those who attended these classes, and have sent me their questions, concerns, and stories, will undoubtedly recognize themselves and the people they know in these pages. Other readers might be surprised to discover that an apparently unique story did not happen to them alone.

The letters in this book are artificial, certainly, not only because they contain references and formal endnotes and are largely the product of my imagination (though my real-life correspondents have on occasion remarked on the same characteristics in my letters to them). The letters are artificial primarily in the sense that they consist of artifice, that is, "devices or expedients," as the Oxford dictionary says, "to trick or deceive." The object of the letters is to use fiction to trick us into truth, which is what novels do. I could never have related the kinds of incidents that are contained in this book were the letters not fictional. The best stories and insights cut so close to the bone of the experience of the men and women whose vocations are shadowed here, that I simply could not have told their stories if I had not possessed the freedom to recast them. Biography, even under the cloak of fiction, teaches us more perhaps than any other literary form — except poetry. Like poetry, biography teaches us most when it can say the least, when the historian's art comes up hard against the intractable mystery of the human heart. Unlike biography, however, sometimes poetry teaches us its greatest lessons in the sheer play of words across the surface of the ordinary. I have often felt that readers of biography and poetry often learn the most when their attention has been diverted from the very things that brought them to the pages of the book in the first place.

Phillips Brooks, one of the best-loved preachers of the nineteenth century (it is said that the entire nation went into mourning when Brooks died, though he is remembered today largely as the writer of "O Little Town of Bethlehem"), once encouraged young pastors to read the biographies of the great figures of the church. He warned however that even the greatest biography about the greatest pastor could ruin a young minister if he or she "read it for the methods of his work." But, if one reads them to discover their spirit, and their spiritual history, biographies can serve the young pastor well.[3] This book is not written to impart methods, but to describe the character, what Brooks called the "spirit," which is the key of all great ministry and which lies at the heart of every great pastor.

Letters to New Pastors

Dear Mal,

Your last letter ends with the question, "What have I gotten myself into?"

I suppose the answer depends on whether you really mean what you're saying. Did *you* get yourself into the mess you're in? Because if you did, then you'd better get yourself out of it. And as quickly as possible.

Pastoral ministry is not a career, Mal, it's a vocation, and if you chose it for yourself, you're in the wrong place. You're only going to do yourself and others a great deal of damage if you stay.

Do you remember what I told you the day you left for seminary? We were standing in the driveway at your parents' house, the August sun bearing down on us. You were so excited to go to seminary you could hardly wait to be on your way. Just before you drove off I said that if there is anything else in the world that God will let you do instead of ordained ministry — anything at all — then you should do it. You looked at me like I had lost my mind.

"You're my pastor," you said. "Shouldn't you be encouraging me to go into the ministry? Don't you love what you're doing enough to recommend it to others?"

And I said, "Of course I love being a pastor. God called me to be a pastor. There's nothing in this world that I'd rather do, not even on the toughest days. And if God is calling you too, then I'm behind you 100 percent. But no one should enter this calling unless God calls."

Remember that conversation?

Malcolm, I still believe what I told you that day. Like Eugene Peterson says, "If you are called to it, being a pastor is the best life there is."[1] Every single day presents new opportunities to participate in the life of God in God's world, to touch people at the most crucial junctures of their lives. What could be a more wonderful vocation than that?

The life of the pastor is the fullest, richest life imaginable. For those called to pastoral ministry, the vocation itself draws us deeper into the practice of the presence of God (as the Carmelite mystic Brother Lawrence put it) than any of us could possibly have imagined when we first took our ordination vows. One pastor likened it to a pilgrim's journey, "if not to the Heavenly City, at least toward the fullest expression of the life that [has] been given us."[2] If Saint Irenaeus was right, centuries ago, when he said, "The glory of God is humanity fully alive," then what calling could be more exciting than the pastor's? Day after day we have the chance to see the glory of God newly awakened in humanity, including our own humanity.[3]

No vocation in the world gives you the chance to exercise such a wide variety of gifts and skills. Reinhold Niebuhr, in his diary from his years as a pastor, tells the story of a young person who argued that "no intelligent person" would even consider being a pastor anymore. Niebuhr replied, "Granted all the weaknesses of the church and the limitations of the ministry as a profession, where can one invest one's life where it can be made more effective in as many directions? . . . Here is a task which requires the knowledge of a social scientist and the insight and imagination of a poet, the executive talents of a business [leader] and the mental discipline of a philosopher."[4]

Ministry is not an easy road. Ministers today are not held in the same esteem as they were fifty years ago. They're rarely seen as the "first citizens" of their towns anymore. Their responsibility is often far greater than their influence. The expectations their members put on them, and they put on themselves, are often unrealistic. And even on the best days there are tough moments, sometimes heartbreaking moments so bleak they cast a shadow over their whole world. I sense that maybe you're discovering at least some of this for yourself.

I've seen pastors come apart at the seams — burned out, worn out, worried out, their health ruined, their families shattered, their congregations split apart — because they could not make peace with the demands and the rewards of this unique vocation. As John Calvin observed, only the call of God sustains us in ministry when the going gets roughest.

If God did not call you to ordained ministry, you really are on your own. And that's not really where you want to be, because you can't do this on your own!

That's why John Chrysostom warned a young friend against entering the ministry in the first place. "The right course, I think, is to have so reverent an estimation of the office as to avoid its responsibility from the start."[5] It is better, as Jesus said, not to put your hand to the plow in the first place than to look back once you've started (Luke 9:62). We should all take this warning more seriously.

So, if you really mean what you said in your question — "What have I gotten myself into?" — then by all means *get out of*

5

ministry immediately before you do irreparable harm to yourself and to others!

I suspect, however, that you don't really mean what you said. You don't believe for one minute that you got yourself into this. You believe God called you to ordained ministry. And know what? I do too. I believe God called you to ordained ministry.

Actually, I think you were the last person to realize that God had called you to be a pastor. Most of the people who knew you best knew God was calling way back when you were toddling around the church building. I've been your pastor for over fifteen years, Malcolm, and I can tell you this for certain: there is a company of witnesses who testify to your calling.

You were probably only eight years old when your church school teacher, Mrs. Harper, came to my study one Sunday after worship to say that she felt sure you were meant to be a minister, and that she intended to tell you so. And she wasn't the only one. Dennis, your youth minister; Mr. Hall, who noticed how much you enjoyed being with people when he took you on hospital visits with him; your friends Bill and Elaine — they all knew your calling before you did.

That's how God's call works sometimes. The Spirit of God speaks through the people of the church, helping us discern the gifts God has given us.

On the day you came to see me to say you believed God was calling you to ordained ministry — you were a sophomore in college, I think — the prayers of a lot of people were answered. You were the only person surprised by the news.

No, I don't believe for a minute that you got yourself into this. Which means you can't really get yourself out of it either. We should both pray for God to show you how to live into and through this calling.

6

Thankfully, the effectiveness of our ministry doesn't depend on us. Our ministries and our callings, like our lives, rest in God's hands. Do you remember the words of the Heidelberg Catechism? "What is your only comfort, in life and in death?" *"That I belong — body and soul, in life and in death — not to myself but to my faithful Savior, Jesus Christ."* This confession is not only for individual Christians. It's also the whole church's confession. *The church belongs — body and soul, in life and in death — not to herself, but to her faithful Savior, Jesus Christ.* Our congregations, our ministries, our programs, our service, our witness, our worship — all belong to God, and are ours by extension. We receive all this that we call "ours" as a gift from God. This is a word of deep, abiding comfort! We're called to a calling that is never our possession. This is God's ministry in God's church for the sake of God's world.

All of which brings me to Mr. Grimsby and Mrs. Thresh, and the other question you raised. That Mr. Grimsby and Mrs. Thresh are driving you crazy is understandable. And normal too. I suspect they'd drive most pastors nuts. Mr. Grimsby's incessant complaining about what you say and do is no doubt irritating (incidentally, he might have a point about the changes you introduced to worship last Sunday — just because he's annoying doesn't mean you shouldn't listen to him). As is Mrs. Thresh's unwillingness to let the young professional women use the church's silver tea service for their weekly meetings. But the kingdom of God is not immune to irritation and annoyance, and the church is not an idealist's abstraction or a utopia. The church doesn't hover twelve feet off the ground. Whatever miracles of transformation and formation God is up to in the church, they happen right where you live and worship, at the corner of Main Street and Seventh Avenue.

You know this. I suspect you've known what ministry would be like all along. The call to pastoral ministry is not a call to secluded meditation. You are not called to be a hermit. In some traditions the pastor's vocation is understood to be a "secular" rather than a "religious" vocation for this very reason. Those of us who are called to pastoral ministry are called to live and serve *as* God's people *among* God's people. Ministry happens in the real world, just as surely as Christ was crucified and raised in the real world.

Pastors and congregations are *God's* people, but we never stop being *people*. The fact that we are human doesn't detract from the divine purposes God has called us to. If the doctrine of the incarnation teaches us anything, it is this. The poet Robert Frost gets at this theological vein when he writes: "But God's own descent / into flesh was meant / as a demonstration / that the supreme merit / lay in risking spirit / in substantiation."[6]

The God who is Spirit became flesh and blood for the sake of the world. The same God calls us, in the name of Jesus, to this wonderful and exhilarating, joyful and confusing, messy and frustrating vocation of pastoral ministry where God's life becomes flesh-and-blood reality among God's people — every day. This is the routine miracle of the church. And just because it's routine doesn't make it any less a miracle. The presence of politics and conflict and misunderstandings and all sorts of odd and ordinary behavior in the church does not mean that God is not at work among these people. It simply reminds us of what God is working with — people.

Saint Gregory was not only a major theologian in the fourth century but was also a pastor in the Asia Minor village of Nazianzus. He described the church as a weird beast that was a composite of all sorts of other animals, "of various sizes and degrees of tameness and wildness." He said the pastor's primary work is to lead and care for this beast, knowing what sort of response is appropriate to each member of the beast's body. He writes, "Since the common body of the church is composed of many different characters and minds, like a single animal compounded of discordant parts, it is absolutely necessary that its pastor should be at once simple in his uprightness in all respects, and as far as possible manifold and varied in his treatment of individuals, dealing with all in an appropriate and suitable manner."[7]

I like Gregory's metaphor, but I'd like to extend it a little. The church is a veritable zoo of diverse beasts. But it doesn't necessarily follow that the pastor is the zookeeper. Sometimes you are, but not always. In fact, the pastor is more likely to be just another orangutan in God's ecclesiastical zoo. Christ himself is the zookeeper, the caretaker, and the veterinarian.

Gregory's comments have been on my mind a lot lately because of what is happening to a neighboring pastor.

Over the past few months my colleague at the Peach Grove Community Church allowed a relatively minor incident to escalate into a serious crisis. His zoo is in shambles as I write this letter. It's a shame too, because he's a pretty decent guy. But I don't know if he'll survive the chaos.

Right after coming to Peach Grove he made several visible changes in the worship service. He moved the sermon in the order of worship. He dropped the confession of sin and the Apostles' Creed. He cut the number of hymns they sing in a service from three to two. And he replaced the bread the worship committee provided for the Lord's Supper (from a recipe that had been reverently handed down in the church for at least eight generations) with unleavened bread. When some of the elders came to his study to tell him they had been fielding complaints for weeks, he told them he was restoring worship to a more appropriate pattern. He refused to budge. Then the fur really began to fly.

Rumors about him spread through the congregation. And problems started to crop up in all sorts of weird places. There were conflicts about the Sunday school curriculum, conflicts about the time for committee meetings, conflicts about the color his wife wanted to paint the walls in the parsonage. Conflicts were springing up overnight about nothing at all — and everything at all.

So my colleague hunkered down in a fortress mentality and pulled up the drawbridge. One Sunday morning he found a note taped to the pulpit. I won't go into what the note said, but it wasn't complimentary. Somebody complained about him to officials in his denomination. Within a few weeks a petition was circulating around the church demanding that he resign. In a church of 250, there were 70 names on that petition. He's been the pastor of Peach Grove for less than a year.

He and I had coffee a couple days ago. He's trying to decide whether to leave or stay. The conversation disturbed me because he repeatedly called his congregation "a clergy killer." Now, I don't doubt that there are churches that are clergy killers out there somewhere, but his church is not one of them. I think he just got himself into a testosterone-induced power struggle with his people. In my experience (and I'm looking back with the benefit of twenty-twenty hindsight), most of the times when the congregation resisted my ideas, they were right, even if the ideas themselves had some merit. Many churches, especially small ones like yours where new pastors come and go every few years, have managed to survive primarily by ignoring or resisting their pastors' innovations. I don't know what my colleague is going to do, but the whole unholy mess seems so unnecessary to me.

One of my seminary profs always said not to change anything major in a congregation for a year or so, at least until you and the congregation have built up a level of mutual trust. That's not a hard-and-fast rule, of course, but I have found it generally true that introducing changes, especially in worship, too early and without gaining broad support for those changes, only serves to undercut the formation of the bonds of trust that are essential for good pastoral ministry to last.

I guess I'm saying all this because I want to draw a parallel between God's calling of you to be a pastor and God's calling of a congregation to be a congregation. God's call is moderated through the voice of the whole people of God. It's never merely private or individual. The Spirit of God speaks God's Word to us, calling us into God's ministry, through the people of the church. But this isn't the end of God's corporate ways. God apparently loves crowds. God continues to speak as leader of the church through the church God leads. This isn't private or individual, either. Church leadership is deliberative. What I'm saying, in other words, isn't just pragmatically true, it's theologically true! The pastor and the congregation negotiate their path together. Together they seek to know the heart and mind of God among them.

The best pastors encourage deliberation among the people. The best pastors respect the movement of God's Spirit in the community. The best pastors help people discover the gifts God has given them. The best pastors help people sharpen their perceptions, deepen their understandings, and exercise the leadership to which God calls them — even (maybe especially) when they don't agree with the pastor.

Someone once said that trust is so precious in pastoral ministry that we ought to spend with care what has been given us. We certainly shouldn't blow it on pet projects and ideas that the church doesn't share our passion for. But I think we can do better than just hoarding the trust we are given. We should try to understand what the people of the congregation are called to become and do as the people of God and then invest the trust they place in us in ways that will bear compound interest. Trust is earned, and it can bear tremendous interest if handled well. Usually the first step in earning a congregation's trust is to show them that we respect them.

Theologically, this means learning as new pastors to honor and adore the Christ who was at work in this church long before we arrived. We didn't bring God with us from the seminary or from our home church. God was at work in your congregation long before your moving van pulled into town. We can't be good pastors unless we are first and foremost disciples, and, as you learned in your basic New Testament Greek class, a disciple is a willing learner.

I guess all I'm really saying (in a pretty roundabout and long-winded way) is that Mr. Grimsby and Mrs. Thresh are God's gifts to you — sometimes irritating and annoying they may well be, but God's gifts nonetheless. Mr. Grimsby wanted his nephew to be called as pastor of your church. You knew that, didn't you? Maybe he'll get over it, maybe he won't. And I suspect Mrs. Thresh is afraid the people who use the silver won't know the saints of the church in whose memory the silver was given, and might not handle it (and, symbolically, their memory) with proper respect. She might see a ding on the silver sugar bowl as a sign of disrespect for people (like her) who have invested so much of their lives in the church. Obviously you've got some negotiating to do with both of these folks. And, if Calvin was right when he said it is ultimately with God that we have our dealings in all of life, then you are also negotiating with God whenever you are dealing with God's creatures, including God's more cantankerous children.

Thomas à Kempis, whose *Imitation of Christ* I have kept on my desk and have reread countless times in the more than thirty years I've served as a pastor, says God intends for us to be edified by all the difficulties we experience. "It is good," Thomas writes, "that we sometimes suffer opposition, and that people think ill of us and misjudge us, even when we do and mean well. Such things are an aid to humility, and preserve us from pride and vainglory."[8] Since no one, according to Thomas, "can live in the public eye without risk to his soul," it is wise always to keep before us God's means to our salvation. God saves us, we believe, through God's calling of us in Jesus Christ. But, as an old friend once told me, there are some of us God can only save by making pastors of us. I wonder, Malcolm, if you aren't one of these.

Sincerely,

Dear Susan,

Please don't misunderstand me. When I said last week on the phone that I am incurably Protestant, I wasn't so much "bragging" (I think that's how you described it) as simply affirming or confessing a reality. In fact, there are times when I say the same thing more as a lament than anything else.

I certainly was not advocating that we live in perpetual reaction against our Roman Catholic brothers and sisters, doing the opposite of whatever they do just so we're not mistaken as members of the same family — as indeed we are (members of the same family, that is). It doesn't do us any good to cut ourselves off from the larger church or to be always reacting to other Christians, like only our little band has it right.

George MacLeod once told the story of a sailor, a latter-day Robinson Crusoe, shipwrecked on a lonely tropical island. When he was rescued many years later, he gave his rescuers a tour of his island home. He showed them his camp, the straw hut he lived in, and not far from his hut, his own little church, where he worshiped each week. Later that same day, as they were walking in another part of the island, the rescuers saw a building that looked curiously like the church that stood near the survivor's hut. They asked him, "What's that? It looks like a church."

"It *is* a church," he answered. "It's the church I don't go to."[9]

The church we don't go to shapes so much of our identity as Christians. The most common litany of my childhood (if we had believed in litanies) might have been: "We don't do that. That's Catholic." For some people it's "We don't do that. That's fundamentalist." Or: "We don't do that. That's what liberals — or evangelicals — or Pentecostals — do." The possibilities are almost endless in the game of defining ourselves by what we do not do or do not believe.

This is not, by the way, always all bad. Sometimes it may be necessary and important and good to say what we aren't, or what we won't do, or what we don't believe. Knowing and clarifying our boundaries, including our faith boundaries, is important in itself. But we can also get into really ridiculous situations defining ourselves negatively.

One of my seminary professors told the story of a small west Texas church he once served as pastor. After years of scrimping and saving, the little congregation built a steeple on top of their church. It was metal, and came to a nice, neat point. But as the pastor and the deacons stood in the church parking lot looking up at their new steeple, they began to scratch their heads and say, "You know, it doesn't look finished. We need something on top of the steeple."

One deacon said a weather vane would look nice. But weather vanes can be expensive, and one good west Texas windstorm might send it sailing toward Oklahoma. One of the younger deacons, inexperienced and new to those parts, suggested they put a cross on top of the steeple.

"No!" the entire group answered in unison. "That's Catholic!"

The pastor solved the problem with Solomonic wisdom. He said, "Just leave it to me. I know what would be perfect."

The next Sunday when they arrived at the church, they saw a beautiful, silver, football-shaped object adorning their steeple.

The deacons said, "It's perfect."

All the people said, "Amen."

And to this day their steeple is topped by a toilet float spray-painted silver, a restroom artifact bearing silent witness to this church's aesthetics and faith — but at least they didn't look Catholic.

I hope I'm not doing that. I certainly did not intend to go down that road. I was only trying to affirm (not brag about) the features that distinguish Protestantism within the larger Christian family. Trying to emphasize that those things distinctive to our various Christian traditions are usually worth preserving, and we'd be poorer if we lost them. In this context I'm incurably Protestant — and Protestant of a certain sort. I have colleagues and friends who are just as incurably Roman Catholic, though to do them justice I should add that they're incurably Benedictine, or Franciscan, or Dominican, or whatever. See what I mean?

It seems to me that it also matters that you, Susan, are a particular sort of Christian. God has called you with your particular gifts, your specific potentiality and your specific limitations, with all your psychological baggage packed and all your spiritual preoccupations in tow, including the very specific and particular spiritual preoccupations that belong to your religious heritage. There's no such thing as a generic Christian, or a Christian in abstraction. Christians are always concrete. We are Christian in particular, maybe even peculiar, ways. The particularity of the Christian way is not merely incidental to the gospel of Jesus Christ. We worship and serve an incarnate God. There's no way to be true to an incarnate God in abstraction. That's why saints are so closely identified with the places where they lived and died.

One community's saint may be another's nutcase. Saint Godric, the medieval hermit saint, was huge in the Northumbrian region of England, for example, where his kindness to field mice and rabbits suffering from hypothermia convinced many of his sanctity, but there are places where he would have been viewed as an eccentric loner. One saint achieved quite a reputation for holiness in his area by living on top of a pillar, while another is honored to this day largely because of his real estate dealings. Somehow in the mystery of God these local saints enrich our common life, reminding us of something crucial about God's calling and gifting of each of us.

The larger church, the body of Christ with its many different members stretching toes to fingertips across time and eternity, is infinitely poorer if we are not concretely who we are, though the most important thing we have to say about ourselves is never about our "denominational distinctives," but about the God who holds us in existence and calls us to follow Jesus Christ. See what I mean?

Sure, there's something faddish and just plain trendy about our society's preoccupation with diversity. But, for the church at least, variety, diversity, and difference are living realities, and they have spiritual significance.

C. S. Lewis, who was fiercely allergic to fads of any sort, once observed: "It takes all sorts to make a world; or a church. This may be even truer of a church. If grace perfects nature it must expand all our natures into the full richness of the diversity which God intended when He made them, and heaven will display far more variety than hell."[10] Of course, it was also Lewis who coined the term "mere Christianity" to affirm that essential faith in Christ that is common to all Christians.[11] I would argue that an appreciation for diversity does not conflict with the faith we share in Christ.

You were asking me how you can defend or justify your commitment to participate in an ecumenical service, to a colleague who rejects any such cooperation. That was the gist of the debate in your ministerial association, if I understood you correctly.

I believe we have a duty to participate in such services. In fact, I believe we have a Christian duty — as distinct from a simply humanistic responsibility as tolerant, so-called enlightened, folk — to respect people who worship differently. By respecting others we respect the God and Father of our Lord Jesus Christ who is at work among us in ways we probably could never imagine. I'm not only concerned about buttressing tolerance here, although intolerance is almost always bad. I'm also interested in confessing faith in Jesus Christ and the ministry of the Holy Spirit through our respect for others.

I remember something that happened several years ago to my late friend Professor James Torrance. He had just participated in a joint worship service of Roman Catholics and Protestants in Belfast, Northern Ireland, and was making his way through the crowd outside the church.

An angry Protestant man confronted him. "How can you, a Scottish Presbyterian minister and Reformed theologian, worship with Roman Catholics?" the man asked.

James answered: "God does not accept us because we offer Protestant worship, or Roman Catholic worship, or some beautiful Anglican liturgy, or 'free prayers'! God accepts us by grace alone, not because of any offering we sinners can make, but only for what we are in Christ . . . for what we are in the person of him who intercedes for us."[12]

The attitude of the pastor you mentioned in your ministerial association (Ernest, was it?), who is unwilling to participate in the community service, is a problem, at least from my perspective. He's the pastor of his congregation, and he feels they cannot participate. Okay. I respect his nonparticipation. And while I disagree with his rationale, I respect it. But while I respect his concern over the integrity of Christian worship, I would argue that it is not we, but Christ, who guarantees the integrity of Christian worship.

Our poor, stumbling, stammering attempts to pray, to praise and adore God, are littered with our own sinful prejudices and preoccupations, our partial understandings and misunderstandings, our distractions and faithlessness. It is only because the Spirit of God gathers up our halting and inadequate worship into the full and perfect worship Jesus Christ offers to God on our behalf that we can say we worship God at all. My confidence is not in *my* faith, but in the faith *Christ has for me.*

I'm not sure it helped anything that you quoted my comments about the high priesthood of Christ at the ministerial association meeting. I suppose it's predictable that Ernest would think I'm just "mumbling abstractions when more practical action is needed." But, also predictably, I could not disagree more strongly with him. The faith of Jesus Christ is not a mere abstraction. Christ's high priestly intercession on our behalf is the most practical thing in the world. It liberates me as a person and as a pastor to rest in what God has done and what God is doing, rather than to fixate on what I do. I may be ranting a bit, but I'm ranting in a theologically appropriate way, right?

Sincerely,

Dear Paul,

What you said sounds good to me. We'll focus on only one subject, as you suggested. Today we'll think about preaching, at least for a while, and see how we get on.

Several years ago a pastor, now retired, took this approach in mentoring me. We had lunch once a month to discuss specific pastoral "themes," as he called them. In fact, he wouldn't go to lunch with me unless we agreed ahead of time on the theme for our conversation. I'd rather not be that rigid, but I think the focus could serve us well.

You said the question you want to tackle first is, What should a preacher read?

I hope my answer doesn't sound glib, but it should be perfectly clear that a preacher should read the Bible. Do you remember that day, not long after you first arrived at your church, that I called you just to check in with you? When I asked you what you were doing, you replied, "I'm trying to pull a sermon out of my head." Remember what I said? "Try getting it out of the text!"

I wasn't just trying to be funny. And I didn't mean to be rude. I was dead serious.

The biblical text is where the sermons are, not in your head. But it takes a considerable amount of courage for us preachers to surrender ourselves and our preaching to the Bible in the conviction that, by the power of God's Spirit, God's Word speaks through these pages.

"It is a fearful thing [not least for preachers!] to fall into the hands of a living God," as the author of Hebrews tells us.

I'll tell you something if you promise not to tell anyone. You know that passage in John's Gospel (21:17-18) when the risen Jesus asks Peter repeatedly, "Do you love me?" and then commissions Peter to feed his sheep? In the passage he then says to Peter, "Very truly, I tell you, when you were younger, you used to fasten your own belt and to go wherever you wished. But when you grow old, you will stretch out your hands, and someone else will fasten a belt around you and take you where you do not wish to go," and the editorial note in the Gospel indicates that Jesus "said this to indicate the kind of death by which he [Peter] would glorify God" (v. 19). You know the text? Well, I've come to believe that the passage doesn't refer only to Peter's arrest and martyr-dom at the hands of the Romans, but it also refers to Peter being bound body and soul to Jesus Christ. I think that's why the pas-sage ends with Jesus saying to Peter, "Follow me." Do you see what I mean? Or am I just allegorizing the passage?

"Feed my sheep," Jesus tells Peter.

Feed them on what?

"I'll show you what to feed them. I'll give you the food they need as they need it," Jesus answers.

This cuts against the grain of what many people think preaching is, though, doesn't it?

A couple years ago a friend who teaches Old Testament at a seminary asked me to visit his class on Ezekiel. He wanted me to talk to his students on what the prophet Ezekiel says about preaching. I confess, although I read through the Bible once a year in my daily devotions, I hadn't spent much quality time with Ezekiel. (Incidentally, Paul, I use one of those programs that lays out a reading every day and covers the entire Bible in a year. Ever tried that? I especially enjoy varying the translations I use: NIV, NASB, KJV, NRSV.) Anyway, I was worried I wouldn't have a whole lot to say to the students about Ezekiel, but when I got to chapter 13 I came upon something I had never noticed be-fore. (Isn't it amazing how that happens, *even with biblical texts we know well!*) One of the things Ezekiel (and Jeremiah too, for that matter) condemns false prophets for is preaching *from their own hearts.* Preaching *from your own heart* is one of the things that makes a false prophet false.

It was like a bolt out of the blue. Suddenly I remembered how pleased I am whenever someone comes up to me at the church door on a Sunday morning and "compliments" my preaching with the words, "That came right from your heart,

Pastor." According to Ezekiel, the only place a prophet's message can come from is the Word of God. If the source of the sermon is your heart, it's coming from the wrong place. The "Word of the Lord" comes upon us, from outside us, from God. The Word of God breaks in upon the preacher. Jeremiah, by the way, "did not question the sincerity of the so-called false prophets."[13] They may have been sincere, but that's irrelevant to the theological issue. They were not preaching the Word of God. This makes sense, of course, when you think about God's calling of the prophets and the apostles.

When Isaiah answers the call of God in the temple, with the foundations shaking and the seraphim in attendance, he responds to God: "Here am I; send me." And then when he hears what the Lord wants him to preach, he asks, "How long does that have to be my sermon?" God's sermon was not the sermon Isaiah wanted to preach.

Saul the Pharisee was no shrinking violet. He was zealous for the Law of God. But he surely could not have foreseen — and would not have chosen for himself — the divine bump in the road to Damascus.

Jesus' words to Peter seem to say that even at their best, the words inspired by Peter's heart would never be more than shifting sand. The church needs something stonier, something more solid, at its foundation. Or, to thoroughly mix up the metaphors again, the sheep need something more nourishing than what Peter could come up with on his own.

Every time I sit down to write a sermon now, and every time I step into the pulpit to preach it, I can almost visualize my hands being tied by the Word of God. I can almost feel my sermon being taken places I would not have taken it on my own.

Over the years I've made a point not only of reading good sermons, but of reading what good preachers say about preaching. Again and again they come back to this same theme.

Paul Sherer once observed that the "Word of God lays hold on the stuff of human existence and reshapes it."[14] When we say that as preachers we read the Bible listening for the claim God makes on our lives through its pages, this is what we mean. As Barbara Brown Taylor says, the Bible interprets us faster than we can interpret it.[15] It seems to me that the biblical text, more than anything else, can save the preacher from the tendency Phillips Brooks warned against, "to preach about Christianity" rather than "to preach Christ."[16] The challenge to which every preacher is called is to get out of the way of the sermon the Word of God wants preached.

This also means avoiding in our preaching anything that gets in the way of the Word of God being heard.

Anything!

One of the disciplines I adhere to is having someone read my sermons before I preach them. I don't always ask the same person to read them, but I always ask the same *sort* of person, someone who cares more deeply about the Word of God being proclaimed than about hurting my feelings. Not long ago I prepared a sermon that I was particularly proud of — which is a pretty good warning signal, by the way — and I asked my friend Scott to read it. You know Scott, don't you? He read the sermon and said the words I dreaded to hear: "The opening story is amusing, and I laughed when I read it, but I think it primarily serves as a put-down to some of your ministerial colleagues and ultimately distracts us from the gospel." I took out the story, of course, and found another way to open the sermon.

Anything that gets in the way of the Word of God being heard has no place in a sermon.

It's the claim of the Word of God that we are listening for when we read the Bible. Which means, of course, that preaching is really just a very public way of hearing the Bible, and the preacher is one among many hearers of the Bible in a congregation. The preacher may not even be the best listener, which is why preachers need to listen to their hearers to understand what they're preaching. In fact, I think the reason some preachers get into trouble preaching what they might call "prophetic" sermons, that is, sermons of a moral or ethical nature, is because they forget they're also hearers of the Word of God, that they also stand under the judgment and grace of God. Preachers are urged by some commentators to overcome this essentially theological dynamic by never saying "you" but always "we." That's good advice. But lots of preachers have the empathetic "we" on their lips while the accusatory "you" remains in their hearts. Know what I mean? When I preach the Sermon on the Mount, I can't escape the fact that I'm a member of the audience and Jesus Christ is the speaker.

Of course, we've probably all seen the opposite tendency too. A few years ago I was at a conference where the preacher took us through a lectionary drawn from Mark's Gospel. Every time he stood up to preach, he read the text from Mark and then tried to convince us that Jesus didn't really mean what he had said.

Some preachers feel an overwhelming compulsion to save the church from Jesus. Whether this is a consequence of a desire to please people or just a general failure of nerve, I do not know. But either way it's deadly for Christian preaching.

Trust the biblical text. Let it be faithfully heard by you and your congregation. Of course we must wrestle with the Bible. Sometimes even argue with it. There are biblical texts I shudder to ponder and psalms I hesitate to pray even in the privacy of my bedroom, much less to preach in public. But I want to hear them for what they are, and listen through them to the Word of God speaking to us.

If we're true to the biblical text, there may be times in church when we can't quite catch our breath because we're so astonished at what God desires of us. What is it Annie Dillard says about the dangers of worship? It's insane to wear straw hats to church; "we should all be wearing crash helmets. Ushers should issue life preservers and signal flares; they should lash us to our pews."[17]

What should we preachers read? Let's start here. Let's read the Bible and just see where that leads.

Sincerely,

Dear Jim,

Thank you for your recent letter. The dean of your seminary, Mac MacBride, is a good friend of mine, and an old one. He and I have known each other since we were in college together. He called me a couple days ago to say that you would be in touch. He seems to think I can be of some help to you as you begin what is referred to these days as "the call process." That's a strange way of saying it, but I'm pleased to help out however I can.

We don't know each other, so I'm a little unsure whether you'll welcome my reflections. Some of the things I'm about to say may appear very critical, though I assure you that I intend them constructively. I have a tendency to say what I mean, so if you don't want to hear my viewpoint, just stop reading now.

Is that fair? Okay then.

At its heart the pastoral vocation is a teaching ministry. I like to think that almost anyone in my congregation could come to me and say, "Why do you do that?" and I would be able to say, "I do that because. . . ." It's sort of like in Deuteronomy 6, where we're told that when our child comes to us and asks, "What do the testimonies and the statutes and the judgments mean which the LORD our God commanded you?" we should answer, "We were slaves to Pharaoh in Egypt; and the LORD brought us from Egypt with a mighty hand" (vv. 20-21 NASB). I'd like to think that a member of my congregation might come to me and say, "What does it mean when you do this, or when you say that?" and I could take that as a teaching moment, and could give a theologically informed rationale for my words and actions.

The reason I'm saying all this is because I want to frame my response to you just a bit. You raised a number of really important and valuable questions in your letter to me, but the way you raised them limits and even undermines your attempts to speak theologically to your people. Your way of conceptualizing the pastoral vocation is thoroughly consistent with the professional and business world, but it lacks the theological groundedness necessary to carry out your teaching ministry as a pastor.

In fact, some of the phrases you used in your letter caught me off guard. You say you want to be sure to "negotiate a reasonably good package with a church," and "to sell" yourself well, and so forth. I know these sorts of statements fly in the business world, but I find them confusing and a little offensive. To be truthful, they're more than a little offensive. They're inappropriate in speaking of the call to pastoral ministry.

Mac tells me you spent over ten years in the business world before attending seminary. I'm convinced that life experience and professional business experience can really serve a person well in the ministry, and I wish more of my colleagues had entered ministry with an understanding of how to deal with budgets and personnel, not to mention organizational leadership. But not everything one learns in life or in business can be applied seamlessly to the pastoral vocation.

Incidentally, I searched your letter in vain for the word "calling" used in connection with what you term your "new job." I know that doesn't necessarily mean anything sinister, and it doesn't mean you don't think of ministry as a vocation or calling, but taken along with your other remarks, it raised a red flag for me.

I think the primary work of the Christian pastor is to bring life, all of life, into theological perspective. It's to help people understand their lives in light of who God is and what God wants of us. This means, at least in part, that we have an obligation to use the right words for things. For example, you ask in your letter how you should go about negotiating your "days off," because, as you put it, "professionals must take care of themselves if they want to stay sharp."

You might be right, but I wouldn't put it this way. How you put things matters. When I think about vocation, God's calling of us in rest, play, and work, I think primarily in theological terms. For example, I don't think a pastor has a leg to stand on if he or she demands "days off." There is simply nothing in the Bible or in the historic teachings of the church to warrant a pastor's negotiating for vacation time, or even a day off. Not in those terms, at least.

But, Sabbath! Ah, now. That's a different matter altogether. The pastor has not only permission but a sacred obligation to observe and teach the Sabbath among God's people.

From the first time it is mentioned, "So God blessed the seventh day and hallowed it, because on it God rested from all the work that he had done in creation" (Gen. 2:3), to Jesus' new hallowing of the Sabbath within Jewish tradition, "The sabbath was made for humankind, and not humankind for the sabbath; so the Son of Man is lord even of the sabbath" (Mark 2:27-28), the Bible treats us to a whole world of theological reflection on what it means to live as human beings in light of who God is.

Abraham Heschel, whose book on the Sabbath is one of the most powerful, beautiful, and moving theological reflections I have ever read, describes the Sabbath as "a palace in time with a kingdom for all. It is not a date but an atmosphere. It is not a different state of consciousness, but a different climate. . . . It is a day that ennobles the soul and makes the body wise. . . . What is the Sabbath?" he writes. "Spirit in the form of time."[18]

A pastor who insists on getting his contractual "days off" is only setting professional boundaries. While thinking about professional boundaries may be important at some level, talk like this may squander a vital pastoral and teaching opportunity. The pastor who by example reminds us of our need for Sabbath rest, by contrast, invites us deeper into God's covenant of life with all creation.

Do you see what I'm getting at? The theological way of talking about humanity's utter dependence on God; our respect for our own limits as creatures, "frail creatures of dust and feeble as frail"; and our reverence for God's creation — this is the language of Sabbath. And this is an explicitly *theological language* because it engages a profoundly *theological reality.*

I know we don't want to get all embroiled in Sabbatarianism again. Absolutely not. That old chestnut is rotten at its self-righteous core. I'm not arguing for a return to legalism. I grew up in a world that did not permit us to attend movies on "the Sabbath," or to play cards, or even to listen on that day to any music deemed "secular," meaning, of course, any of the music we wanted to listen to. In my house Dizzy Gillespie was fine on Mondays, but not on Sundays.

I remember a pastor our church had when I was a child who chastised two of my friends for playing tennis on a Sunday. When they told him they noticed that he dug in his flower garden on Sundays, he quickly defended himself. "Digging in a flower garden is okay, because you can wear a shirt and tie while you garden. Anything you can do while wearing a shirt and tie is okay on the Sabbath."

No, I'm not arguing for a return to that attitude. But when we gave up on the specifically theological language of Sabbath, we severed the concepts of holy rest and recreation for the soul from God's creative purposes.

Do you see what I'm saying?

Something similar could be said about your remark, "I want to make sure I sell myself really well, put on my best face, and make myself look as good as I can for the churches I interview with."

The way some congregations search for a new pastor does resemble a beauty contest. I'll grant you that. I can almost see the contestants arrayed along a catwalk in bathing suits (clerically appropriate bathing suits, of course), discoursing on how they plan to seek world peace and church growth if chosen.

You are certainly not the first seminarian (or pastor, for that matter!) to use the language of sales in speaking of the call. But I don't think it serves you or the church well. As a pastor and a congregation interview, they are seeking to understand whether God is calling them to enter into a union. There's something like courtship involved, and that calls for us to look and behave our best. But the process is subverted and the potential union is doomed if the pastor and congregation do not really get to know one another along the way. The whole process of mutual observation and conversation opens the way for spiritual discernment between the potential pastor and congregation. The interview is really an occasion to listen to an Other beyond each other, to hear, beneath the various expressions of hope and dread, excitement and regret, the very voice of God that must be present if a pastor and people really are called to live with one another.

I keep coming back to marital metaphors when speaking of pastoral ministry, but I think they fit especially well. No two people are perfectly compatible in marriage. There are real limits to our compatibility, and we must strive to overcome them. It's also a bad idea at the beginning of any marriage to think, "I love you. And as soon as we get married, I'm going to change you." Reminds me of that Broadway play: *I Love You, You're Perfect, Now Change*. No, it's much better to develop the relationship through mutual faith and honesty.

The relationship with a congregation is the same way. When you interview with pastoral search committees, you and they are best served by trying to get to know each other as prayerfully and honestly as possible. Do you and the congregation share a sense of what it means to be Christian? Do you respect one another's faith and life as authentic and authentically faithful? Is there the potential for enduring trust to develop in this relationship?

These are the most important questions, and they are essentially theological questions.

Most of the time when pastors "sell" themselves, congregations end up getting buyer's remorse. Don't sell yourself. Be yourself.

I'm not sure how to say this, so I'm just going to follow my instincts and charge right into it. I am struck by the fact that you seem to bless uncritically our culture's reverence for money. I know I've entered dangerous territory here, because money seems to be about the only really sacred thing in contemporary culture, and like all sacred matters, it is guarded by the taboo of silence. A pastor told me years ago about a marriage counseling session he had once in which he led a couple into a searching examination of every aspect of their lives, from talking about their childhoods and their children to talking about the most intimate details of their sex lives. One week he asked them to talk about how they used money. Immediately they protested, "If you insist on talking about what we do with our money, we're quitting counseling. That's private!"

As dangerous as it may be to bring up this subject, especially with someone I don't know well, I feel I have to. Again, this is a theological issue. It's an issue that Jesus had a lot to say about.

I recently read John Chrysostom's sermons on Jesus' parable of the rich man and Lazarus (Luke 16). Chrysostom (you read him in seminary, I trust) preached seven sermons on wealth and poverty. I'm not sure I've ever read anything that calls into question so radically so many of our society's assumptions about money, possessions, and property. Karl Marx is Tinkertoys compared to Chrysostom.

Chrysostom sees many of the things that we seek — physical comfort and financial security, luxury and even simple pleasures

— as potentially dangerous to our spiritual health. Why? He says they obscure a proper understanding of the relationship between God and God's creation. According to him, all our goods are not our own; they belong to God. And because they belong to God, they belong also to others. How we handle God's possessions has eternal consequences.[19]

There is in your letter a respect for "your" time, "your" possessions, and "your" gifts that I'm relatively sure our society would find healthy and positive, but I'm not convinced is healthy from a Christian perspective. You might complain that I'm reading too much into the way you say things. And you might be right. I might be overreading what you're saying. But I want to take your comments seriously. That's at least a part of what it means to respect others: taking what they say seriously. And taking your words seriously, I'd say, as a word of warning, that none of the things you possess is yours at all.

This all feels a little too preachy to me, so let me shift to the first-person singular. I do not share my time with others. Together we share God's time. I do not share my resources with others. The resources that are in my bank account are God's, and others have a claim on them too. The gifts God gives me aren't mine by right. I hold them in trust, and I can keep them only by sharing them.

Classically, in Christian thought, the category under which we think about these things is stewardship. God the Creator entrusts the world and its bounty to our care. And our spiritual health as Christians relates directly to how well we exercise our office as caretakers of what belongs to God.

As you approach the interviews you've scheduled with pastor search committees (apparently you're interviewing with several congregations), I would simply remind you of the calling to which you have been called, and encourage you to see these interviews less as auditions than as opportunities to bear witness to the abundance of God. Too often we pastors miss the opportunity when negotiating our pay to remind our congregations what it means for us to live as stewards. We act instead as though we are just negotiating a contract.

Of course, one of the main things that saves ordained ministry from the corruptions of the professional agents who dominate sports and the entertainment industries is that the public doesn't value what we do as highly as it values the work of quarterbacks and movie stars.

Thank God for small favors, I suppose.

Does this mean that you do not have a responsibility to negotiate a salary package that takes good care of your family? Of course not! You have this obligation. But the theological dimensions of our vocation do raise the stakes. We aren't just negotiating a salary package, we're engaged in the pastoral office of teaching. We're teaching stewardship to our congregations using our own lives as a model, for good or ill. The question is, *what* are we teaching?

Again, your questions are important and good questions that I wish everyone entering ministry would ask. Please forgive me if I've spoken too frankly. And give my best regards to Mac when you see him.

Sincerely,

Dear Dorothy,

Thank you for your letter. I do indeed remember you from the seminary class I spoke to last spring, though mercifully I don't remember much of what I said that day. I recall you coming up after class and saying you wanted to be in touch with me after you received a call to a church — which apparently you have.

Congratulations!

The story you told me is rather scary. Yes, to answer your question, I have heard of things like this happening. Be careful. And, no, I don't think you overreacted, at least from what you told me. You *should* take seriously a threat of violence such as the one you received. The woman's husband seems to have blamed you for the independence his wife is claiming, since you have been counseling her. Whether or not he'll make good on his threats, I think you were right in calling the authorities, especially since he told you on the phone that he was on his way to the church "right now to take care of you for wrecking his family."

This incident makes your question, about how much and what sort of counseling a pastor should do, much more than merely theoretical. But I do need to back up a bit to answer it. I suspect you would get a lot of different answers depending on whom you ask. All I can do is give you my perspective.

I think a pastor should have lots of training in psychology and in pastoral counseling, but I don't think pastors should do a great deal of actual counseling, at least not the kind of long-term therapeutic counseling that is the bread and butter of psychologists and other full-time therapists. Certainly you are the primary resource for your congregation when it comes to grief and crisis counseling, just as you are the primary conflict mediator for your church. But long-term marriage and family counseling, and the kind of therapy that people engage in for personal growth and enrichment? Leave that to full-time counselors. I recommend that you develop a list of such counselors to whom you can refer your people. Incidentally, this why it's so important to be well trained in psychology. Along with giving you a deeper general understanding of our humanity (which is important in itself), a training in psychology also qualifies you to spot the particular problems the various members of your church may be having and know which counselors will serve your people best when they approach you for help. Knowing how and when to refer your people to psychologists and other therapists is a tremendous therapeutic service. The reason I don't do much pastoral counseling is not because I think it's unimportant. It's quite the opposite. I think pastoral counseling is so vital that I want to limit my engagement in it, and I want to responsibly fulfill my pastoral role in relation to it.

Obviously, there are also geographical considerations to take into account. Middlesborough is in the middle of nowhere. I looked it up on the map! You're probably two hundred miles from the nearest counseling center. So, it is likely that you are the first line of defense for your congregation when it comes to counseling needs. And maybe the second, third, and fourth lines as well! That means you may need to make pastoral counseling a larger part of your ministry than I would, living as I do in a city. But, even in Middlesborough, I'd be cautious about how much and what sort of counseling I would do. And for two reasons, both related to your vocation as a pastor.

First, counseling requires a lot of time and energy, and time and energy are limited resources for pastors. Until someone's actually been a pastor, there is no way he or she can imagine how busy pastors are. Someone said being a pastor is like being a dog at a whistlers' convention. Responsibilities stand on virtually every corner desperately trying to wave you down, as though you were a passing taxi at rush hour. Some responsibilities are simply closer to the core of pastoral ministry than others. Preaching, teaching, providing leadership to your congregation, engaging the culture around you with theological integrity, vision, and a sense of mission — these are at the very core of the congregational pastor's vocation. Providing pastoral *counsel* is also very important, but it's very different from providing pastoral *counseling*.

A good pastor is prepared to enter into healing conversations of all sorts — spiritual, emotional, and physical — with members of his or her congregation, and with others. Some of the most crucial of these conversations occur in the most unlikely of places, at the most untimely of moments. Anywhere, anytime a pastoral conversation *can* happen, a pastoral conversation *will* happen. I've been pulled aside in the produce aisle of the supermarket and told things that would make the cabbages blush, and have been expected to respond pastorally while the radishes looked on. But such conversations — and they are real pastoral conversations demanding thoughtful pastoral counsel — are not the same as formal therapeutic counseling sessions.

When I do make the decision to engage in pastoral counseling, whether with a member of the congregation or with others, I generally limit the number of sessions to three or four. If more are needed, I refer the person to a therapist who can carry on a longer-term counseling relationship. It is not fair to the congregation at large for their pastor to tie up the lion's share of his or her time and energy with a small group of "clients."

Second, counseling and pastoral leadership both require

clarity of roles, and if you are trying to be both counselor and leader, there are bound to be muddles and mix-ups, some potentially tragic. I learned this the hard way — and not quickly either. I have come to believe that congregational leadership is ordinarily the primary pastoral role. I have a responsibility to the whole congregation that I should not jeopardize by confusing my roles.

This is especially tricky with counseling, because therapy involves certain interpersonal dynamics — like transference and countertransference — that can prove devastating to pastoral leadership. And it is so easy, *so* easy, to betray a confidence, or appear to betray a confidence, when preaching. And even an appearance of this sort can ruin relationships and undermine your leadership in the church. I have known situations when a pastor did a magnificent job as a therapist, but by the end of the counseling process (it was marriage counseling) the couple left the congregation because they wanted to make a fresh start with another pastor who didn't know so much about them.

There are all sorts of temptations and pitfalls in counseling. I remember a couple that came to me for marriage counseling. I visited with them twice before referring them. After three weeks with their pastoral counselor the wife came to my study requesting that I talk to them again. I suspected they were feeling some creative tension in the therapy, and I refused to talk to them about anything related to their counseling. They tried everything, from flattery to threats, to get me to be their counselor again, but I resisted. Instead I encouraged them to talk to their therapist. If I had talked to them, I would probably only have released the stress they were feeling, stress that had the potential to motivate them to change their marriage for the better.

I don't think you can get too much training, incidentally, especially in dealing with grief and crises, but also in detecting various personality disorders and mental illness. Gregory of Nazianzus described the pastoral vocation as "the art of arts and science of sciences," in which the pastor serves as a physician of the soul.[20] While I think the most therapeutic thing a pastor can do for a congregation is to preach well and lead among the people of God, it also makes sense to understand the human situation as well as one can.

By the way, you mentioned a concern about "time management." In my experience, most pastors who have difficulty "managing their time" have failed to gain a deep sense of what should occupy their time as pastors. The problem is not so much failing to master certain techniques related to the clock, it's failing to discern what should guide their days and determine their priorities. Time management per se is simply a matter of good administration, and you can learn most of the techniques for that from a good book while sitting by your fireplace on a cold winter night.[21] But the deeper issue of how to determine what should occupy your time is a matter of vocation that must be worked out over years of experience. This is a spiritual issue. Not every demand on our time and energy should be given the same weight. Determining what is most important is a matter for spiritual discernment. And spiritual discernment of a particular sort — that of a pastor who is thinking about how and when to respond specifically as a pastor.

There have been times when I rushed out the door in response to a phone call from a member of my congregation, and other times when, after receiving such a call, I stayed put. And from an outside perspective, both calls might have sounded very much the same. But, as pastor, I weighed a variety of issues in determining my response to each person's need. I made a judgment call. Every pastor must learn how to do this because, in some sense, all of ministry is really about discernment. Discernment is a gift, but I've never known anyone's discernment to be infallible, and almost everyone's discernment can be sharpened and deepened if you work at it.

Of course, determining how and where to invest our time is not unrelated to the issue you raised about counseling. Unfortunately, there are no final, absolute answers in the back of the textbook. We are given broad guidelines (in the Bible as well as in the vows we take at our ordinations) that instruct us generally over the long haul. But, as in so many other areas of pastoral ministry, we must negotiate our way in prayer, in reflection, and in conversation with the community of faith, including our colleagues in ministry.

Sincerely,

Dear Mal,

So, you hate "church politics"!

The problem with hating church politics, my friend, is that there is no church without politics. You know this. You grew up in the church. Your parents have served as elders in my congregation for more years than I can remember.

I'd like to challenge your understanding of church politics, though, because when you said the phrase, I heard a distinctly derisive tone in your voice.

If the church didn't have politics, it wouldn't be a group of people trying to work out how to live together. Because that's what politics is: people working out their common life, people negotiating their values, beliefs, and aspirations *and* the varying degrees of influence necessary to promote the values and beliefs they hold precious and the aspirations they think are worth the work. Granted, the church is more than just a group of people trying to work out how to live together, *but it is certainly no less than that.*

Incidentally, the conflict at Peach Grove Community Church has reached its climax. My colleague resigned yesterday. I told you about him in my last letter — the one who started making major changes to the worship service right after he got there. Anyway, he came by my house late Friday afternoon and told me that he intended to tell the congregation on Sunday. It's really a sad business. When he talked about the hopes he had going into this call, it was almost like listening to a person lamenting a failed marriage. So much hope simply evaporated. No one won.

As he sat in one of the chairs in my study, tears welling up in his eyes, he said, "If I had known back in seminary what I know now, I would never have gone into the ministry."

"What," I asked him, "do you know now that you didn't then?"

"It's all so political," he said. "I thought I would be the spiritual mentor for a community of Christians, that they would respect my word, that I'd have some authority. But the only important thing was how well I got along with the power clique and the rich people."

As in war, the first casualty in a church fight is often the truth, and I fear my colleague's pain and anxiety have made a liar of him. It may be a cliché, but it's true: *the people don't care what you know unless they know you care.* The fight in his church was not just about control and power; it was a disagreement over respect. The church never was convinced that their pastor respected them. And I have to confess, I don't think he did. The whole conflict was not only avoidable, it was reparable right up to the end. A real mess!

Your disparaging words about the evils of church politics (and I don't dispute that some church politics are wicked, by the way) and the troubles my colleague has experienced have brought to mind a paper you wrote while you were in seminary. You sent me a copy. I dug the paper out of my files. It's one of the many benefits of being a pack rat.

Isn't this a paper you wrote in a church leadership course? It doesn't say so, but I think it is.

You write: "Politics is morally neutral human social behavior. Like power, it may be used for bad or good, but it is not necessarily evil *per se.*" (By the way, I hope you don't preach the way you write papers; this is pretty dry stuff!) You say the word "politics" comes from the Greek word *polis,* and that according to the Greeks, "politics concerns the inner relations of the *polis,* the city, the community." If this is true, then politics is not a necessary evil for the church, it is simply its natural condition.

I agree with your argument, but the real question is: Do *you?*

I wouldn't say that we should engage in the worst aspects of political practice in the church — pandering to the lowest common denominator to win popularity, promoting partisanship that splits congregations into warring factions, placating those who throw their weight around, producing propaganda (I guess they call that "spinning" these days), toadying, blackmailing, and so forth. But I do think there is a kind of politics that is appropriate to the life of the church.

Isn't it politics to work with others, including people of influence, to create a more livable community? Isn't it politics to seek the goals that are achievable now while not forgetting what we want to achieve in the long run? Isn't it politics to try to build bridges between people who may be able to agree on essentials though they would never agree on certain other things? Isn't it politics to shape our words diplomatically so that we can be heard even when tempers run high? Isn't it politics to pay attention to the interests and perspectives of the congregation, even when we don't personally share all their interests and every aspect of their perspective?

I suppose I'm reacting a little to those pastors who think they can be more spiritual than God, who are like the "pious people" Joseph Sittler once described, who walk through the world holding their noses, "as if God's creation somehow smelled bad and we ought not get too close to it."[22]

Surely there is such a thing as the politics of God. And where should that kind of politics be practiced if not in the church? God speaks God's eternal Logos in and through the life of particular people in particular congregations creating God's own *koinonia.* I'm sort of paraphrasing what you said when you paraphrased Aristotle.

Isn't this what the church father Basil of Caesarea meant, at least partly, when he spoke, toward the end of his treatise on the Holy Spirit, about the conflicts over doctrine and practice then raging in the church?[23] Bernard of Clairvaux, Martin Luther, John Calvin, Dietrich Bonhoeffer, Reinhold Niebuhr, Dorothy Day, Martin Luther King, Jr. — all of them seemed to understand that there is a politics that is life giving as well as a politics that is soul stifling.

I would be grieved, Mal, if you were involved in the latter, but I am worried that you resist the former. It's a lot easier, of course, to reject politics out of hand than to try to walk this tightrope of taking seriously all the conflicting needs and interests and concerns and values of your members, all coming from diverse perspectives. It's tough balancing politics' redemptive potential and its potential abuse, to be both faithful to God and deeply involved in human society. And yet how else can we remain true to the incarnate God?

Jim Wallis recently mourned the fact that "politics has been reduced to the selfish struggle for power among competing interests and groups, instead of a process of searching for the common good." He says, *"We can find common ground only by moving to higher ground."*[24] I hope you're willing to do all you can to redeem the church politics of our time, because if politics is left only to those of few scruples, we can hardly be surprised when it is unscrupulous.

Ah, well, forgive me if I'm getting too *aerated,* as the old Yorkshire farmers used to say, but I'm grieving the loss of a colleague.

When I came into my office this morning, the church secretary was all abuzz about the "big news" from Peach Grove Community Church. She had heard all about my colleague resigning already. I just sighed, shook my head, and walked into my study. There's nothing left to do but cry.

When the relationship between a pastor and a congregation breaks down, so many people get hurt. I just wanted to be by myself for a few minutes. As I sat at my desk, my eyes ran across the bookshelves, and came to rest on a book I have read so often the pages are literally falling out of it: Niebuhr's *Moral Man and Immoral Society.* I took down the book and read from it.

Allow me to paraphrase what Niebuhr reminds me of today, as I watch my neighbor's ministry come tumbling down: Our common life is both the basis for and the enemy of the fullness of life we seek. Politics is the arena where conscience and control meet, where ethics and power collide, and where we must work out the tentative and uneasy compromises that make it possible for us to live together.[25]

I finally thought of the title of that sermon you were asking me about on the phone, the one by Arthur John Gossip: "But When Life Tumbles In, What Then?" Let me know what you think when you read it. It's in his collection of sermons, *The Hero in Thy Soul.* I love the epigraph Gossip chose for that volume, the passage from Thomas Carlyle, about awakening the hero that slumbers in our souls. Good stuff, and not entirely unrelated to church politics.

Sincerely,

Dear Dorothy,

The conversation you had with the young woman, Alice, reminds me of something I read years ago. In fact, your comments made me go back and read it again. It was in the *Shepherd of Hermas,* an ancient book of instruction from the early church. I read it when I was a young pastor, as part of my postseminary learning strategy.

I decided, not long after I graduated from seminary, to treat the writings of the past like a huge treasure chest. I started by reading right through the apostolic fathers — Clement of Rome, Ignatius of Antioch, Polycarp, the *Didache,* and the *Shepherd of Hermas.* I got hooked on the wisdom of the church, and just couldn't stop.

Well, anyway, while reading the *Shepherd of Hermas,* I was especially struck by the instructions on how to discern true and false prophets, and how to test the spirits we encounter to determine which are from God and which are not. You see where I'm going, don't you?

Alice (did you say she is considering a call to pastoral ministry?) told you that in her view the Holy Spirit is synonymous with "the quiet voice that she hears within her heart telling her what to do." And when you asked her the question that I frankly would also have asked her, "How do you discern the difference between your own will and the will of God when you hear this voice?" she said, "If I feel really compelled to do something, then I know that it must be God speaking." I thought your response was both pastoral and perceptive. You told her that, in your experience, the more compelled or driven you feel in a situation, the more you suspect that it is you and not God that wants you to do the thing.

The reason I bring up the *Shepherd of Hermas* is because of two things it teaches about the testing of true and false spirits — and both things are countercultural, even to the prevailing Christian culture in the churches you and I live in.

First, every spirit is not automatically from God. For a lot of people, simply to say that something is "spiritual" is enough! They seem utterly unaware that the spiritual realm is as crowded with virtues and vices, goods and evils, godly and wicked options as the emotional realm is. And the physical realm and the intellectual realm too. We have a responsibility as pastors to test the spirits to determine whether they are good or bad.

Second, we should never confuse our own spirit with God's Holy Spirit. We are creatures. God alone is Creator. God's ways are higher than our ways, as far above us as the heavens are above the earth. Alice's statement may appear pious to Alice. But to me it sounds profoundly arrogant. She's making it very hard for anyone to question her "strong convictions" because the fact that they're strong means they're from God. She's insulating herself from precisely the kind of "testing of spirits" that Christians must do to be responsible to the Spirit of God. (By the way, I find it odd that so many Christians these days seem to equate a person's willingness to talk knowingly about God — especially about all the things God is for and against — with faithfulness. I rather think that reticence and reverence are connected.)

I suppose what worries me most about Alice is that the same rationale she uses to justify her belief that God is calling her to be a pastor (because she feels compelled by her inner voice to do so) could be used to justify all sorts of other things, even very, very bad things, if that's all she has. Again, I agree with you. So often it's my compulsions (sometimes my apparently "holy" or "righteous" compulsions) that God seems to have to keep in line. In fact, I've come to believe that every time I have the compulsion to put on my Superman outfit and rush to the rescue, it's probably not God talking but my ego. I've just been hooked emotionally, and my natural rescuer is engaged, which of course plays nicely into my pride.

So how do we "test" the spirits? How do we discern what is of God and what is not? It's a messy and complicated business. We are warned in the *Shepherd of Hermas* against manipulative prophets who mix a little truth with falsehood to lead us astray.

And, Lord knows, we can do that to ourselves just as easily. What I wish Alice had said when you asked her how she tests the spirit that guides her is: "I compare what this spirit tells me with the Word of God," because the true Spirit of God never contradicts the Word of God. I wish she had said, "I ask the community of faith, the living congregation of God's people, to hear the testimony that I believe comes from the Spirit," because the Holy Spirit is the living breath of the body of Christ, and it is through the voice of the church that we discern the voice of God among us. I wish she had said, "I run to the gospel of Jesus Christ to compare what I have heard inwardly with what Christ himself said and did," because the true Spirit is the Spirit of Christ, and the true Spirit partakes of the character of Christ. As *Hermas* observes, the divine Spirit produces the same meekness, calmness, honesty, modesty, openness, and reverence we find in Jesus, while the false spirit is puffed up and arrogant and immodest, indulgent and deceitful. The false spirit boasts of its power, but it is really empty and impotent, while the true spirit (I love this image) is like a tiny hailstone that falls from a thundercloud. It's powerful because it comes from above.

I'm curious where you think your relationship with Alice will go from here. Do you think she'll pursue ordination? I suppose I'm especially curious because when she came to your study, she began the conversation with you by saying that she was "inspired" to consider ordained ministry as a calling because she had been so blessed by your ministry that she considers you a role model. But as soon as you began to ask her to reflect critically on her calling (something everyone who is called must do!), she seemed to turn on you, and to threaten you. Did she really say that if you don't support her moving forward with ordination, she'll ask her father to withhold his financial pledge from the church?

There is a quiet, private calling we hear from God in our hearts. And there is a deep sense of providential calling we may sense as we survey our gifts and begin to think that perhaps God has given us the aptitude and talents necessary for ordained ministry. But there's something else as well, and that is the confirmation of this calling that must come through the voice of God's people. We believe that all three are necessary because we have found that God's Spirit says nothing privately to us that God's Spirit does not ultimately confirm through the community of faith in which the Spirit works. Again, we're talking about testing the spirits here. What is it Ebenezer Scrooge says to the ghost of Jacob Marley when the ghost asks his old friend why he doubted his appearance? "You might be a bit of underdone potato.... There's more of gravy than of grave about you!" Well, I seldom take old Scrooge's side, but he was right to test his own private encounter with the spirit world. The church has consistently held that we can have more assurance that God is speaking to us if what we think we have heard is confirmed by the testimony of the community of faith.

I think it's also important to remember that not every calling is to ordained ministry. Did you explore that with her? We are called to follow Jesus Christ. We are called to all sorts of vocations. The calling to ordained ministry is only one of many sorts of callings, and I have known a lot of people who assumed that when God called them, they must "go into the ministry." Sometimes they have realized this after years of frustration as pastors, and they have left a ministry to which they were never called.

My thoughts and prayers are with you as you continue these conversations.

Sincerely,

Dear Paul,

Of course I didn't mean the Bible is the only thing we should read!

I'm surprised you'd think I was advocating (as you said) a "retreat from the wealth of intellectual and imaginative resources we have in common with all of humanity." Of course I'm not! George Herbert's sage admonition stands. "The Country Parson's library *is* a holy Life." Indeed so! A life without books is hardly worth living, for me at least. Though I haven't always thought so.

Until I became a pastor, I confess that I wasn't much of a reader at all. As a child I read some adventure tales — *Treasure Island* and *Call of the Wild*. I read *Huckleberry Finn* and *Robinson Crusoe,* and more comic books than I can count while lying across the bed in my grandmother's house during those long summer afternoons when I was supposed to be napping.

I read what I *had* to in school, especially in high school and college. And I read theology and biblical studies in seminary. But I didn't really fall in love with reading *for the sake of reading* until I started preaching every week. A neighboring pastor, whose preaching I admired, told me early on that I should read more fiction and poetry, so I asked him for a few suggestions. Once I started reading really good fiction and poetry, I developed a voracious appetite that has never gone away.

My original motive, as you might imagine, was simply to get

illustrations for sermons. Soon, however, I learned that the reason to read great books is not to get illustrations, but to reach a deeper level of human and theological understanding. Wisdom is the quarry we're seeking when we read, not just good stories to make a homiletical point. I raced through novel after novel, reading Flannery O'Connor, Graham Greene, Walker Percy, William Faulkner and Ernest Hemingway, Isaac Bashevis Singer, Chaim Potok and Elie Wiesel, Nathaniel Hawthorne and Herman Melville. I soon discovered that the reason I hadn't really gotten into fiction before that was because the fiction I was reading was just not compelling. In fact, most of it was boring. So I traded in pulp fiction for Dostoyevsky, and I've never been bored with my reading again.

In a sense, as a pastor I rediscovered the level of reading I had taken for granted in childhood when I read Robert Louis Stevenson and Mark Twain.

So, why is this level of reading so valuable?

I'll tell you by borrowing an argument I came across recently. Michael Dirda, the editor of the *Washington Post Book World,* says: "A true literary work is one that makes us see the world or ourselves in a new way . . . which is why literature has been defined as writing that needs to be read (at least) twice. Great books tend to feel strange. They leave us uncomfortable. They make us uncomfortable. We are left shaken and stirred."[26] Lest you protest that this has nothing to do with pastoral or theological or faith matters, let me add that words in general imitate the Word in particular, the Word of God, the Word who is God. So it isn't far from novelist Marcel Proust's reflection on his reading of John Ruskin, the English art critic (Proust wrote, "The universe suddenly regained infinite value in my eyes"),[27] to theologian Karl Barth's observation that the Word of God strikes human history like a bomb shattering everything we took for granted about existence, forcing us to rethink everything anew.[28]

Much the same is true for poetry. There are few things in print worse than bad poetry. But good poetry . . . well, good poetry reveals a whole new world! As I began to explore good poetry, at first I read lots of Robert Frost and Carl Sandburg, both of whom I had memorized as a schoolchild. In time I moved out into unfamiliar waters, reading William Blake, E. E. Cummings, T. S. Eliot and W. H. Auden, Gerard Manley Hopkins, John Donne, George Herbert, Seamus Heaney, and John Ciardi, with whom I became acquainted because of his translation of Dante's *Divine Comedy,* Sylvia Plath, Philip Larkin, Anna Akhmatova, and Philip Levine.

My advice to you as a new reader of poetry is to find a poet just beyond your present level of understanding, and read that poet until you really, really get it. Then move on to another poet. You'll never lose the ones you come to understand, and you'll always be pushing yourself further into deeper water. A bad poem is by definition a poem whose meaning you can exhaust the first time you read it. A good poem grows with you, new meaning emerging the longer you live with it. This explains why Shakespeare is great.

What I said about distinguishing good poetry from bad is true for hymns too. A bad hymn is one you can understand fully the first time you sing it. A good hymn unfolds itself over time throughout our lives, taking us deeper, showing us new things about God and the life of faith. It's crucial for pastors to know this, because a congregation's theological understanding will never rise above the level of the hymns it sings. And this explains why Isaac Watts makes a better diet than Fanny Crosby. And, please, don't get me started on the hymns so popular in trendy churches of all sorts and persuasions today that praise us and the furniture instead of expressing our adoration of God. I hold to the apparently outmoded idea that a hymn or spiritual song or chorus should consist of a strong text grounded in praise and thanksgiving, adoration and amazement in the presence of God. Even the music should take us deeper, demanding more of us, reminding us of the infinite qualitative difference there is between us and God and the incredible act of condescension it requires for God to meet us in mercy and grace. Incidentally, have you seen Jeremy Begbie's *Theology, Music, and Time* and Calvin R. Stapert's *My Only Comfort: Death, Deliverance, and Discipleship in the Music of Bach*? There's also a fascinating study by Julian Johnson, *Who Needs Classical Music?*[29] What a great time to be thinking theologically about the music and the texts our congregations are singing, especially when you factor in the Taizé and Iona music! Yet, what a difficult time too! Whether they are engaging in traditional, contemporary, or blended worship models, most of our churches deserve so much more than they're getting. I'm not arguing for liturgical elitism by arguing for depth. I'm simply pleading for our contemplation and worship of God to correspond to the awesome majesty and wonder of the God we worship. Never forget that choosing hymns for worship is as crucial a task of proclamation as preaching itself.

Okay, I've got that digression out of my system — for now. Let's get back to reading.

These days my reading list includes lots of new names along with the old. I'm reading Tolstoy's *Anna Karenina* right now. But I also read contemporary writers (and near contemporary writers too) like Penelope Fitzgerald, Ron Hansen, Peter Taylor, A. S. Byatt, Peter Ackroyd, John Irving, Francine Prose, Gabriel García Márquez, Jim Crace, Julian Barnes, Thomas Lynch, and Jane Smiley.

Recently a Methodist colleague — a district superintendent, in fact — told me he doesn't want pastors who read, he wants pastors who learn from experience. It's a false choice, and if taken to its logical conclusion, it forces us into a really dangerous situation. The fact is, if all you have to draw on is your own little experience of the world, you simply can't learn enough to be a great pastor, no matter how well you utilize your experience for learning. But if you read, you can multiply your experience exponentially. A reader can live a thousand lifetimes, and every pastor needs at least that much experience. As Joseph Sittler said, "I would be a poor person if the only things I knew were what I have found out for myself. Through great poetry and drama and essays I have experienced things that my own bracketed life never permitted me to experience firsthand."[30] Years ago I came across a passage from Thomas Carlyle that I tacked to one of my bookshelves: "All that mankind has done, thought, gained, or been; it is all lying in magic preservation in the pages of books." It's all there. All we have to do is retrieve it!

What was it that Martin Luther said? "Only a fool learns only from experience."[31]

One of the pastors I admire most, Bill Enright, for many years the senior pastor of Second Presbyterian Church in Indianapolis, says one of his seminary professors challenged him to read a new book every week. He's come close to doing that for decades now, and it shows in his preaching, in his conversation, in his whole life.

"What do you mean, it shows?" I can almost hear you asking. Just this: it's clear when Bill poses a question that he brings to bear on that question a staggering mass of knowledge and wisdom drawn from the best minds in the world. He lives in conversation with these minds, allowing what they have learned from their experience to be added to his own lively experience of the world around him. Recently I had a conversation with him about stewardship and finance. Within a few moments our lunch table was (metaphorically speaking) crowded with dozens of very informed people offering their perspectives, their arguments and counterarguments, on the subject. No pastor is so rich in ideas and experience that he can ignore the treasury of wisdom that stands on the bookshelves of our world. And this is no less true for the truth that can be found in fiction than it is for the information and thought we find on the pages of nonfiction books.

I began this letter by praising George Herbert's admonition, "The Country Parson's library is a holy Life." Herbert makes a similar point to what my Methodist friend did. He values one's own experience over secondhand knowledge derived from books. Herbert writes: "He that hath been sick of a Consumption, and knows what recovered him, is a Physician so far as he meets with the same disease, and temper, and can much better, and particularly do it, than he that is generally learned, and was never sick."[32] Now, I revere Herbert, and I honor the truth he expresses here, but I would add that the physician who ignores the practice of other doctors and the experiments of medical researchers is a poor practitioner of the medical arts. Our people suffer from diseases and distempers of spirit and psyche that are far beyond any single minister's individual experience and competence. The whole wide world of spiritual and emotional maladies that afflict our people requires an army of scholars, pastors, saints, and doctors to experience, to understand, to diagnose and treat. I, for one, am grateful that I have Flannery O'Connor and Nathaniel Hawthorne and Søren Kierkegaard to help me diagnose the sickness unto death that passes itself off as a counterfeit form of righteousness, and that I have George Eliot, Graham Greene, and Walker Percy to help me discern a robust spiritual health that lies under an apparently deathly pallor.

You mentioned in your letter a book you are reading about Walker Percy, Dorothy Day, Thomas Merton, and Flannery O'Connor, but you didn't mention the author or the title. Please send me the details when you write again. I must read this!

Sincerely,

Dear Susan,

Thank you so much for your letter. I'm sorry it's taken a couple days to get back to you. I just returned from a mission trip to northern Mexico (and am now preparing to visit our youth at their summer church camp).

Every year I make the mistake of thinking that life will be slower around the church in the summer months. But we don't slow down; we just shift gears. In some ways it's even busier than during the rest of the year, especially when you factor in youth camps, vacation church school, conferences, and the way we share duties when various staff members take their vacations. Anyway, I came to your letter this morning, and wanted to get back to you right away.

I am very sorry to hear that things have taken such a nasty turn in your ministerial association. It's a sad day when Christians, especially Christian pastors, cannot find a way to love one another, or at least to grant one another respect, even if they don't agree with one another's doctrines.

As you may know, I served in a town with Reverend Dickenson many years ago. Back then he was personally active in the ministerial association, and he was very involved in the community, although he wouldn't allow his congregation to do any sort of joint projects with our church. I always considered him a friend. In fact, we fished together quite often. I can't help but think that what happened to his daughter played some part in producing that "hard, cold shell" you speak of that seems to have formed around his heart. I'm sure you know all about it — her becoming a member of that cult, and the tragic circumstances surrounding her death. Personally I cannot imagine surviving the pain that he and his wife endured. I suppose Dick is just coping as best he can, but it is sad, and I am very sorry. I don't know, but it seems to me that he has now allowed his grief and anger, and his fear of people who believe differently, to focus on you, as though you are somehow the "enemy." I have to tell you that I find it hard to imagine him standing up in the association meeting and calling you the kinds of names he did. I can't imagine the courage and grace it took for you to sit there and take it without responding in kind.

The questions you ask about why it is difficult for people to deal with difference are, obviously, rooted in the recent ordeal you've been through with Dick. I'm tempted to restrict my response in this letter to the pastoral issues that underlie Dick's comments. And there *are* pastoral issues. In abundance. They range from the difficulties of simply communicating with those who do not share our language, and whom we are tempted to discount or exclude because they're different and their language and customs are strange to us, to the fears and anxieties that surround many people these days in light of terrorism and what some have called a "clash of civilizations."

But I think I'll address the larger issues anyway. If you don't mind. I don't know if my thoughts will cast any light on what you've been facing, but maybe they'll at least help me dig through some of the issues I've been dealing with as a pastor in an increasingly diverse city where it is less and less likely that your neighbor will share your faith, many of your values, and even your ultimate hopes.

Coming to terms with diversity, it seems to me, is one of the greatest challenges we face as pastors and as Christians. But I'm not as convinced as you seem to be that the only choices we have are either absolutism or relativism. (Maybe I'd feel different if I had just been attacked by a colleague, as you were!) Both options appear to be variations on the same tired old theme.

The absolutist says, "There's one and only one answer to every real question regarding faith, values, and hope. I know that answer. And everyone who doesn't agree is wrong — maybe even evil." I think it was the absolutist that Henry Hardy had in mind when he said that "English country vicars" are simply "the more acceptable face of the kind of enterprise that in other contexts abets political violence and hatred."[33] Whether the absolutist excludes others because they fail to agree with him, or is a liberal-minded absolutist willing to overlook the errors of others and call it tolerance, he or she still believes there's one and only one answer to every real question.

The relativist lives on the opposite end of the same long street. The relativist might say that all roads lead to the same destination (a patently foolish and false idea, if ever I heard one), or that the right answers are ultimately hidden from us so we must muddle through in ignorance, making do with the best answers we can come up with. But the relativist believes, nonetheless, that if a question is a real question, it has one real answer, even if we cannot know what it is.

It's hard to say which option is worse. The absolutist approach seems to end at the doors of the gulag or the concentration camp, where everyone who disagrees with "my" way, the "right" way, is locked away forever or gassed. The relativist approach ends at the doors of hell itself, where the most sacred obligations and values, the most treasured hopes and dreams and beliefs of humanity, are ultimately met with smug cynicism and are reduced to trivialities. I am reminded of what Thomas Shepard, the Puritan preacher, said about toleration: "To tolerate all things, and to tolerate nothing . . . both are intolerable: but 'tis Satan's policy to plead for an indefinite and boundless toleration."

Neither approach takes seriously enough the variety that God has woven into all creation, the extravagant, overflowing *multi*-verse (as William James called the universe) that God has created. And as a pastor and a Christian, I want to find a way to take seriously the deep diversity of God's own eternal being (Father, Son, and Holy Spirit), and to think through God's own diversity to understand the breathtaking diversity of God's creation. You see, if God really were the singular, bare, windowless monad some philosophers take God to be, then it would make sense that all reality, creation, humanity would be just as singular, just as isolated and distant from others, just as bare and windowless. But God is not. The God revealed by Jesus Christ is richly complex — a mystery. (No! *The* Mystery.) God has God's being as holy Trinity, the triunity of Father, Son, and Holy Spirit.

In some sense God is a particular relationship, an eternal relationship: the Father is the eternal well-being of being who brings all things into being; the Son is the eternal self-giving imageless image of the Father; and the Holy Spirit is the eternal life and love God the Father and God the Son share with one another, and with all creation. This triune God, whose being resides in the mystery of multiplicity in unity, created the world and humanity from the depths of God's love and life, and placed on all creation the indelible stamp of God's own triune character. God created all things and endowed all things with a measure of that freedom that resides at the core of God's sovereign character. This surely is the great and terrible and wonderful story we hear again and again in the Bible: a story of God's grace that precedes and makes possible God's law; a story of God's mercy that redeems us from every fall; a story that illustrates repeatedly that God loves freedom more than safety.

All of which means that there are many, many real questions that may have more than one right answer. And this is true not simply because we are ignorant or sinful, but because God and God's creation are far bigger and deeper and more complex and more wonderfully mysterious than any one answer can express. And the various people, communities, societies, and cultures that encounter and try to make sense of God and God's vastly rich creation will inevitably see and experience things in vastly different ways, and bring their understandings and faith to expression in vastly different ways too.

That certainly doesn't mean that all roads lead to the same place. Some roads are dead ends. Some roads cross each another. Some roads lead up, and some roads down. Some run parallel, and some run on top of each other, like blacktop laid over an ancient cow trail. But just because a good question has two very different answers, it doesn't mean one of the answers is necessarily wrong.

You began your letter by asking me how to tolerate someone whose views you truly disagree with. And how do you have a relationship with someone who hates what you care most about? These are personal, not abstract, questions. And they deserve a personal answer. But they also deserve an informed answer. I'll take a stab at it.

There are different kinds of toleration. And some forms are intolerable. But I would say of toleration, generally speaking, that it is a baseline, minimal response to difference. Bernard Williams once observed, "The difficulty with toleration is that it seems to be at once necessary and impossible." This, he said, is especially true of religious toleration. "We need to tolerate other people and their ways of life only in situations that make it very difficult to do so."[34]

Toleration can be as minimal as simply putting up with someone else's mistakes. I've known "tolerant" people who were condescending to others. I've even known "tolerant" persons who had little or no respect for the convictions of others. On the other hand, tolerance can be as radical as welcoming into fellowship a person whose views you condemn, and committing yourself to hear and, as much as possible, to learn from that person's convictions. Tolerance can take the form of forbearance or of acceptance, if not of the other person's views, then at least of the other person. Tolerance, in my view, is not identical with that anemic complacency or apathy that many people in our society have toward the beliefs and values of others. Tolerance assumes that something (an idea, a goal, an aspiration, a practice, etc.) worth fighting over is at stake. Risk is involved in tolerance; and it can cost. At the minimal end of the tolerance scale, tolerance may cost me only a bit of time and patience. But it can cost a great deal more. Tolerance can exact a price in life and treasure, including the treasure of reputation, if goodwill is betrayed.

In a sense, though, I'd say toleration in itself is never really an adequate Christian response. We must love others and recognize in their differences the possibility that we are coming face-to-face with the image of God in them. We must show hospitality, welcoming the stranger as though the stranger is Christ himself, no matter how "strange" the stranger may be. And we must forgive, a concept that must begin where even understanding falls short. All these Christian virtues go well beyond toleration, while all of them might see toleration as a starting point.

I don't know if I told you this, but a few weeks ago I had a terrible argument with a member of my church. I cannot imagine now how in the world I let things get so heated. It just so happened that I left town the day after our argument. I was driving that next day, a Sunday morning, and as the usual time for worship approached (the holy hour of 11:00 A.M.), I found myself in a small town. I literally pulled into the first church parking lot I came to, walked into the church and sat down. I had never been in this church before, and in fact had never even been in a church of this denomination before. The preacher was preaching on the topic "Is Toleration a Christian Virtue?" You may be interested in his answer. He said, "I don't know if toleration is a Christian virtue. But I do know that humility is, and I know forgiveness is. Whether or not we are willing to tolerate the differences of others isn't really the question. We are called to discipleship by a God who guaranteed us only that if we follow him, we will receive a cross. That's it! Next to what the cross demands of us, tolerance is small potatoes."

As soon as worship was over, I found a phone and I called the church member I had argued with. I swallowed my pride, and asked for forgiveness.

Your situation is, it seems to me, somewhat different. Maybe you don't need to ask for forgiveness (I don't know. I'm just making that assumption), but you do have the opportunity to forgive. Whether Dick accepts your forgiveness or not — well, that's not in your power. What is in your power is to forgive. Compared with that, as the preacher said, "tolerance is small potatoes."

Sincerely,

Dear Malcolm,

Obscure! Erudite! Abstract!

What do you mean? Simply because I quote Basil of Caesarea, John Chrysostom, and Gregory of Nazianzus, all of a sudden what I say is irrelevant?

What can I make of your comment that you're "allergic to such dusty tomes" except that, because the Christians I quoted lived long ago, you don't even think they're worth remembering? And no, I'm not displaying my "academic" credentials by quoting people like Chrysostom — though I'd also emphasize that there is a valid place for academics and scholarly callings in the life of the church. But it's not "academic" for people of the church to remember the saints who have gone before them. If anything, it is merely *churchly* to revere those who long ago built up the household of faith in which we worship today.

Good grief! Has contemporary ministry become so arrogant that it treats "the church at rest" as disposable?

I want — no, I *need!* — to hear the voices of that chorus of witnesses who have lived the life of faith before we were born. I suppose it's not a very popular idea these days, but tradition matters. Not traditionalism — the hidebound, unquestioning, uncritical reverence for "the way we've always done it" — but tradition, the deep-flowing springs of wisdom and faith, the living legacies of whole communities of God's people in the past welling up and bringing refreshment to God's people today.

I agree with G. K. Chesterton, that at its most basic level, tradition is merely "giving votes to the most obscure of all classes, our ancestors. It is the democracy of the dead."[35] But they're not just "the dead," not according to our faith. "If we live, we live to the Lord, and if we die, we die to the Lord; so then, whether we live or whether we die, we are the Lord's" (Rom. 14:8). How arrogant for us to assume that because we enjoy the historical accident of being alive today, we're wiser than Basil of Caesarea, who lived in the fourth century. We need Basil's wisdom, and we need it now.

Well, you've gotten my blood up, friend, but it's just because your comments are not uncommon. The contemporary church, at least in my neighborhood, is like the goose that wakes up in a new world every morning.

Recently I read a book on pastoral ministry — there's no need to say by whom — that said the crisis facing the church in our time (and, honestly, I can't remember which crisis the person was referring to) is the greatest the church has ever faced. Not only is this historically inaccurate bunk, it whips up anxiety about the state of the church, and anxiety is the worst enemy of wisdom. Anxiety makes a poor counselor. Anxious people tend not to make good decisions; they just make desperate choices. The voices of Basil, Chrysostom, Gregory, Julian of Norwich, Martin Luther, John Calvin, and many, many others give me perspective. They remind me that the church is far larger and grander and deeper and more extensive than my meager individual experience of God.

In one respect, though, you might be right. It does seem that those who possess the scholarly (let me use that word rather than "academic") vocation tend to bear the greatest share of the burden for reminding the church of its deep traditions. Sometimes it seems that Christian scholarship is meant to function as the long-term memory bank of the church. Even fairly old churches seem to have a corporate memory of only twenty-five or so years, essentially a generation. Some suburban churches (and you know I have served a suburban church now for many years), with their frequent turnover of members, whether due to church shopping and church hopping or the transient nature of middle-class society, can't remember back even ten years. Christian scholars can and should remind us that the really big and really important conversations about God and faithfulness stretch back for hundreds, even thousands, of years.

A pastor once told me about an experience he had while adjunct professor at a seminary. He said that of all the courses he taught, the one that seemed to have the most profound effect on students, the one able to change their perspective most, was church history. "Most people," he said, "simply assume that all Christians and all churches have looked and thought and acted exactly like them through all the ages. Church history showed them the amazing possibility that God's people can be both faithful and different from our own narrow experience."

Let the saints vote, I say. Let them lobby their hearts out!

I must run. The nominating committee is meeting in a few minutes, and I'm never late for *that* meeting.

Sincerely,

Dear Jim,

Thank you for your very kind words, and for the spirit in which you received my previous admonitions. You're a good sport, because I do tend to be pretty directive in my opinions and advice. That's one reason I don't do much counseling. After re-reading my letter to you, I almost didn't send it. Not knowing you, I feared I was taking some liberties (and undoubtedly I was) in exhorting you so directly.

Mac e-mailed me a few days ago to say that you and he had talked about the letter and that you wanted to continue our conversation. Perhaps we'll be able to continue it in person someday.

Now, to your follow-up question about observing what you call your "boundaries" as a pastor. You asked me, "What do you do as a pastor if something comes up on your day off? Do you go ahead and take off that day, or do you cancel your day off?" As I said before, I think you're on firmer ground if you think in terms of Sabbath, not days off. But even so, it seems to me you have to be very clear and very flexible. So the answer is: it depends.

A friend, the pastor of a busy suburban church, received a call a few weeks ago from a member of a neighboring congregation. The man needed a pastor to bury his father, an elderly man who had died following a stroke. My friend asked if his own pastor was available. "No," he said. "The funeral is scheduled for Friday, but he takes Fridays off." My friend told the man she would have to talk to his pastor first, and would get back to him right away. She called her colleague, and he confirmed that he had refused to do the funeral because it was on his day off. She asked if he would permit her to do the funeral in his place. He said she was welcome to do so, and she made the arrangements.

When she talked to me, she was furious. "I understand the need not to burn yourself out," she said. "But to refuse to do the funeral for a member of your congregation simply because it was on your day off? Substitute another day off that week! Reorganize your schedule! But don't deny to serve as pastor to your people just so you can sleep in!"

On the whole I agree with her. There are times when the needs of our people outweigh our needs for self-care.

Am I saying that burnout among pastors is not a problem? Am I saying that every need of the people outweighs our needs? No, indeed. I do not believe it honors God to work yourself into an early grave.

What I would argue for, however, is a rethinking of the pastor's life, so we can see its theological significance. If we are to provide leadership among the people of God, we need to recover the spiritual heart of pastoral ministry. We need to live lives that breathe in and out naturally. This may require us to deprofessionalize our thinking about vocation. Rather than needing inactivity to recuperate our powers of self-reliance (that's the idea most of us have of a day off; it's a professional entitlement that allows us to escape from the demands of others), God calls us to a kind of life in which solitude and community work in concert, both providing opportunities for recreation and service.

Marjory Bankson has said, "The concept of call assumes we are spiritually linked with others and with creation, whether we like it or not. . . . We separate in order to recognize that we are related — not only to each other but to God."[36] I think this idea flows naturally from the idea that God, the Father, Son, and Holy Spirit, created humanity to reflect God's own trinitarian community. We are created to be in relationship, and if we short-circuit this relatedness, we burn out.

Does this make sense?

In other words, burnout is not a matter of overworking; it's a matter of underrelating, or relating poorly. The question is not whether you interrupt your day off to bury a member of your congregation. That way of seeing things assumes that your purpose in the church is to provide professional services, and that you're entitled not to provide these services at certain times because of the contract you have negotiated. Rather, the question is a matter of your identity, who you are in relation to your people, and what God has called you to be among them. Identity and vocation are never merely matters of contract; they are matters of covenant.

For me, burying my people is the most painful aspect of pastoral ministry. One day I said this to another pastor, a very close friend. She agreed, but then she added, "But I don't want anyone else to bury them." That's a real pastor talking. Community requires a nexus of mutual obligations. And the life we live together in community costs us dearly. Sure it does. It costs us tears and sorrows, worries and regrets. But the life we live together also sustains and nourishes us.

As an introvert, I need time alone. I need solitude or I'm not much good to anyone, especially myself. I become irritable and short-tempered if I don't have time alone to restore myself. Often this is time spent listening to music, exercising, reading, or all of the above. And I need such solitude virtually every day. I am foolish to wait until I'm run-down to rest. Just as I would be foolish to stay awake night after night until I crashed with exhaustion every few days.

Extroverts need time in groups of people for restoration, to gain energy, and to process ideas. They too need to pay attention to the natural rhythms of their lives. They cannot put off indefinitely the regular, normal necessity of being with others. To think of pastoral ministry as a calling is to think, first and foremost, of how God uses who we are for God's own ends. And this takes us back to a subject I touched on in the previous letter: the pastor's observance of the Sabbath. As I said before, while the pastor does not have a theological leg to stand on in negotiating a "day off," the pastor has a sacred duty to observe and teach the Sabbath.

Humanity believes, arrogantly, that the world belongs to us, and is vain enough to imagine that we are indispensable. The emptiness of contemporary culture reduces people to commodities and consumers of commodities, and quantifies every unit of time economically. In contrast, the Sabbath teaches us that time as well as space belong to God, that we depend on God for every breath of life, and that we would fall into nonexistence but for God's sustaining care. Our humanity is not reducible to one-dimensional descriptors (like the tag "consumer") because we are made in the image of God, and made in the image of God as we are, we are created to reflect the character of God.

Sabbath is rest of a particular kind. It's a memorial to God's creation and for the re-creation and restoration of our spirits. Sabbath reminds us that we are called into creation, into stewardship of God's creation, by the God who created all things. It also reminds us that the need for God-directed rest is woven into us as God's creatures.

While the mentality of the "day off" requires us to vacate our work space in order to recharge, the spirit of Sabbath demands that we perceive God at work in the midst of space by honoring the time God has hallowed. The Sabbath reminds us that our souls are claimed in time by the eternal.

Because we are Christians, Sunday, the Lord's Day, the first day of the week, has new meaning, certainly. In some sense every Sunday is the day of resurrection and Easter kicks off every new week. For pastors it is sometimes the busiest day we face. Even as Christ came to fulfill the law and the prophets, Christ fulfills the Sabbath. We rest in Christ. Christ is God's Sabbath for us. Christ leads us into that Sabbath rest that he gives us. Christ does not abolish Sabbath, nor does Christ do away with our need for holy rest.

As pastors, we have this remarkable opportunity to live in such a way that our people can learn their human dependence on God and can experience in Christ that power of restoration that God alone gives. We can do this by observing Sabbath as Sabbath (not as a secular day off) in our own lives, and by keeping the Sabbath holy, set apart.

Which returns us to my friend and the pastor who wouldn't do the funeral on his day off. I think he should have done three things. First, he should be observing Sabbath, and not taking "days off." Second, he should honor the Sabbath explicitly by calling it that and by making it a day for spiritual, emotional, and physical restoration. The Sabbath is not a substitute for living a sane and blessed life every day, however. Sabbath extends its influence into every day of the week, redeeming all the time we live, blessing every day's labors and rest in the name of God. Sabbath teaches us to respect the rhythms of rest and labor, solitude and community that make life worthwhile. Third, he should have honored the life of the community to which he is called by doing the funeral. That's what I think, anyway.

I hope this makes sense to you, and look forward to hearing what you think.

Sincerely,

Dear Paul,

I really cannot thank you enough for the book you sent me. Yes, I know the shop where you bought it — it's not far from Norwich Cathedral. We happened on that same bookshop last summer when we were visiting England. And no, I've never seen this book before, nor do I have any idea who Arthur W. Robinson, D.D., was, though I have to tell you his official title, "Vicar of Allhallows Barking by the Tower, Examining Chaplain to the Bishop of Wakefield," sounds like something right out of Wodehouse.

I take it you read the book before you sent it to me. I have to say it is really interesting. For example, chapter 2, where the author summarizes the message of the chapter with these words: "'Force is not an attribute of God.' We must co-operate. In what sense Grace does not make life easier."

The author's reflections in this chapter correspond quite closely with the concern you raised about the difficulty of understanding certain poets. I'm happy, incidentally, that my remarks about George Herbert inspired you to begin reading his poetry. I know he can be rather difficult, but the efforts required to understand a great poet are returned with interest. (Incidentally, your confusion over his poem "The Windows" might be cleared up by knowing that "brittle crazy glass" means stained glass, and the word "anneal" refers to the process of heating that produces the glass. So, the poem is actually about the way the preacher's own life becomes his or her real sermon as God's story is made manifest in that life through the crucible of existence and the struggle for holiness.) You probably want to find a new critical edition of Herbert's poems, something that has good footnotes, just to help you along.

Anyway, you imply in your letter that if something is godly and good it should not be so hard to do, that grace should clear away the roadblocks. Where could you possibly get such an idea? This wonderful book you sent to me speaks directly to your concern. Robinson says, "Gifts do not relieve their possessors from the necessity of hard work. 'Genius,' in the oft-quoted definition, 'is an infinite capacity for taking pains.' It is the merest delusion to suppose that anything really great has ever been achieved without effort."[37] That's what Robinson means when he says, "Grace does not make life easier." He applies this insight directly to preaching, quoting "Dr. Liddon," who when he "was asked to give some lectures to younger men about preaching, he refused, declaring that he 'could only tell them to take pains.'"[38] Grace, like genius, then, becomes for Robinson "an infinite capacity for taking pains."[39]

If ministry is a practice or a collection of practices, nothing could be clearer. Anyone who has ever been a musician knows this to be true. Some time back I saw a film on B. B. King, the blues guitarist. He was giving a workshop at a jazz conference. One aspiring young jazz performer asked King what advice he had for him. He told him to practice his scales, even if a pretty girl was waiting outside the house for him.

You and I have been talking about the books preachers ought to read, and Robinson's general advice about the grace of "taking pains" certainly speaks to the kind of work we have to do to understand poets like Herbert and Blake and Auden. But this leads me to explore another area of reading the pastor should not neglect: first-rate biblical and theological scholarship.

It's so easy, as a pastor, to join the lax and lazy refrain of those who have abandoned serious study and the reading of serious scholarship, chanting, "I am too practical to read theory." Of course, most of the time it's not "theory" that puts us off; it's the difficulty of the material, the challenge of new ideas, the discipline required to read the best scholars. I'm not sure every pastor has to be a scholar — though I've known some extraordinary pastors who were also first-rate scholars, and whose congregations benefited mightily from their scholarship. But I would argue that all pastors ought to be open to scholarship and ready to learn, if not for themselves, then at least for their people's sake.

Recently I had the pleasure of participating in an installation service for a pastor friend in Atlanta. The preacher was Tom Long. You mentioned how much you enjoyed the books on preaching Long wrote when he was at Princeton. As you know, he now teaches at the Candler School of Theology. Do you know what he told us in his sermon? He said the greatest heresy of our age is not atheism; it is superficiality. You know what? I stood around after the service and listened to the people who came by to shake Tom's hand, and the thing I noticed was the number of laypeople who told him how grateful they were for what he said. They agreed. It reminds me of another story I've heard Tom tell. After he preached a sermon at one evening service, he invited the people to share with him any message they might like for him to take back to the seminary. An elderly lady came forward with a simple and direct message: "Take us seriously."

There are times when I feel as if we, as pastors, are trivializing the church to death. Whether preaching, or shooting from the hip in response to questions our people raise, or writing books that promise too much and deliver far too little, we so often dole out sound bites when something more is needed. We suffer, as one very funny pastor put it recently, from a "profound superficiality." I feel like the cartoon character Pogo when he said, "We have met the enemy, and the enemy is us." The problems our people face, the problems our world faces, are deep and real and serious, and they deserve deep, real, and serious responses from us, thoughtful responses, informed, knowledgeable, and wise responses. John Updike, in a book review, once commented on the quality of the thought of a well-known Christian philosopher. He said something that stung me, as a pastor, because I knew he was right. He said this thinker would never have been taken seriously if his audience hadn't consisted primarily of pastors.[40] When our people say, "Take us seriously," they are asking us, their pastors, to take our vocation more seriously too, a vocation that once set the gold standard for thoughtful, critical reflection.

With this thought in mind, I want to return to your question: What should a preacher read?

The answer: Everything that brings God's world into clearer focus, that's what a preacher should read.

A preacher should read broadly and deeply, and not superficially. Why? Because he or she reads for others. You know the old saying that a pregnant woman is eating for two? Well, the pastor is reading for a lot more than two! He or she is reading for a whole congregation, a whole community, sometimes a whole society. As a pastor you read, you reflect theologically and critically, you muse on and puzzle over what you read for the sake of your people.

This extends even to preparation prior to entering ministry, to life in seminary. The pastor in training is seeking to learn for the sake of all those he or she will teach and preach to and lead for years and years to come. In a sense, sitting beside the seminary student in that class on Bible or theology are the children and adults, the young people and the old, all the people that student will pastor in the future.

The same thing is true when we read. Curled up in my reading chair at home, I am reading with my whole congregation looking over my shoulder. They are always present with me in my study.

Whenever I think about this aspect of our vocation, I am reminded of a poem by Seamus Heaney. It's one of his earliest, and one of his most famous. He's musing on the vocation of the peat digger, his father, cutting into the peat, opening the ground. Soon you are aware that the poet is talking also about his own vocation, cutting into the ground of life with his pen, digging deeper and deeper. Nothing in creation is foreign to the preacher's curiosity, nothing that is true knowledge is out-of-bounds. Deeper and deeper we are called to dig, for the sake of our people, who week after week deserve the best we can bring them from the pulpit, for Christ's sake. Grace, as Robinson said, doesn't make this easier. If anything, the demands of God's grace make this task bigger and more significant.

Harry Emerson Fosdick once said that nobody comes to church with the burning desire to know what happened to the Jebusites. That's true, and scholarship that goes down deep and comes up dry isn't edifying. Nor should scholarship per se be exhibited in the pulpit. I find it distracting when a preacher rattles on endlessly about the significance of the aorist in a particular Pauline verse. But a poor use of scholarship does not excuse ignorance. The lives our people live are fraught with real dangers, intractable difficulties, deep sadness, muddles and challenges beyond measure, and a yearning to understand what it all means. We should take all the pains grace demands to attend to their needs.

Thank you again for the wonderful book.

Sincerely,

Dear Dorothy,

Not only do I believe that there are false and true prophets, and good and bad spirits, but I also believe that the pastor's calling must be understood as a spiritual endeavor. Our vocation is to contend at the level of the spirit for the health and wholeness of our people (and ourselves).

This is why the *Shepherd of Hermas* (and the other apostolic writings I recommended in my previous letter) is not just of interest to antiquarians. It should interest pastors also. If we are to be true to our calling, we have to do the hard work of testing spirits — and testing ideas, concepts, values, beliefs, commitments, and all sorts of other things spiritually. We have to test anything that would seek to take possession of the human soul. And, no, I wasn't just speaking metaphorically about the darker side of psychological processes when I talked about bad or evil spirits, though I do think psychopathologies and sociopathologies could both be characterized generally, in some sense, as spiritual issues. (By the way, I was saddened to hear that the young woman you wrote about has withdrawn from fellowship with your church rather than open herself to the discernment of others in the process of candidacy for ordination. I'm sure this must have been painful to you as her pastor.)

Richard Baxter, in his *Reformed Pastor,* says, "The subject matter of the ministerial work is, in general, spiritual things, or matters that concern the pleasing of God and the salvation of our people."[41] This means, at least for me, that the pastor is attentive to the whole life of his or her people at the most profound level, the level of the spirit. Whether we call this "spiritual direction" or "pastoral nurture" doesn't make any difference. What's more important is that we understand that the development of spiritual disciplines, including corporate worship, Bible study, prayer, and the cultivation of personal reflection, is not an optional extra in the pastor's life and daily ministry. Nor is it optional for the pastor to be spiritually accountable to others in his or her exercise of this, the very core of pastoral ministry.

What we sometimes forget is that exercising "spiritual" disciplines relates to our lives at the most ordinary level. In the most day-to-day events. Like when that annoying man — is he up to no good, or clueless, or (shock!) maybe just an open, friendly person sharing his happiness? — stops by your table in the cafe for the third time in a morning to tell you an "amusing" story that amuses only him, and you begin to wonder if people at the other tables are beginning to wonder if you're a little batty because you treat him with respect. Like when your favorite television program is interrupted by a knock at the door by a young person seeking signatures for something that really does matter, but you resent the person for intruding on "your time" at home. Like when the voice of a loved one begins to grate on your nerves like fingernails on a chalkboard (for no particular reason), and you discover that turning the other cheek may have more to do with listening to the complaints of a member of your church than with military service. Sometimes we think spiritual things are inevitably trimmed in stained glass. Nothing could be further from the truth. The greatest challenges in the spiritual life occur amid the most mundane activities and relationships of life.

Helmut Thielicke, in a book entitled *A Little Exercise for Young Theologians,* tells beginning seminary students that all real theology is prayed theology, reminding them that Saint Anselm's famous ontological argument for the existence of God is actually written as a prayer.[42] I really don't find it hard to think of academic theology as an act of prayer. What I sometimes find very hard, though, is to really, consistently think of pastoral ministry as prayer. Why? Because ministry requires a continual engagement with people, that's why. I find it infinitely easier to extend Christian charity and generosity of spirit to Kant than to the church organist, and no matter how frustrating I may find Barth's statement on the *vestigia trinitatis,* it's nothing like the frustration I feel when the nursery worker calls at the last minute — *again* — to say that she is running late. If ministry is an act of prayer, then all matters great and small are put in a whole new frame, and life (all of life) is a lot more complicated than it appears.

The great dangers in ministry (as in all of life) so often occur below the surface. We see that part of the iceberg that shows above the waterline, and think we're keeping the ice a safe distance from our boat, but we don't notice the damage being done to the hull below the waterline by that part of the iceberg (the much larger part) that we cannot see. Often we don't realize that we're in spiritual danger at all until we begin to sink. The spiritual struggles of ministry mostly happen below the surface, in the subtle attitudes and the motives, in slow smoldering resentments, in stirrings of righteous indignation, in small betrayals, in disappointments and suspicions and impatience, in the emotional strains too "insignificant" to mention.

A small wound inflicted long ago festers unseen in the heart; an unkind word once said is never forgotten. And so often the pastor is the only one who has the opportunity to teach how to forgive when forgiveness itself seems inexcusable, not so much because the one who caused the pain needs to receive forgiveness (though the person does), but because the one who will not forgive will suffer the pains of hell until he or she has learned to pardon. One person may exult in private triumph at the expense of another, which is bad enough, though the real danger may be in the heart of the one triumphed over, who cannot let go of being wronged, whose rightness can in time consume his or her soul. The pastor so often is the one who must examine the wounded heart, who must find a way to convince the broken heart to accept healing.

Pastoral ministry is a spiritual matter, from start to finish. There's never a time, by the way, when we are off duty — not off *this* duty, anyway. In private conversation as in public proclamation, you remain the pastor, and you must remain aware of the claim this office, this role, this calling makes on you.

Speaking of public proclamation: Wasn't it Baxter who said that preachers who aim their sermons at the broken heart will seldom miss the mark of the gospel? I think he said something like that, though I don't remember where. Surely this is true. But *how* is it true? A pastor steeped in the school of the Spirit knows that any sermon aimed at the broken heart must originate in a broken heart — in the broken heart of the pastor who bears his or her own regrets, sins, loneliness, his or her own small, and perhaps large, betrayals of those he or she loves. The pastor longs to hear the word of grace alongside all the other broken hearts waiting for that word from his or her lips. I've always felt that the sermons that have the best chance of being heard are those where the preacher is a hearer too, where the preacher is allowing the Word of God to address both preacher and people in the same breath. But ultimately any sermon that aims at the broken heart of humanity must know God's own broken heart. Elie Wiesel, the Nobel laureate, and surely one of the great souls of humanity, was once asked who the most tragic figure in the Bible is. God, he answered. I cannot read the parable of the prodigal son without thinking of his remark. This surely is the parable of the grieving father.

In your first letter to me, Dorothy, you mentioned that you are on your third career, that maybe you can give the church ten good years before you retire. I believe you're off to a great start. But you said something else that saddened me, though I didn't respond to it then. You said you had wasted forty-eight years of your life before saying yes to God's call. I think I know something of what you mean by those words, but I don't believe the life you lived before accepting the call to ministry was a waste. With God, even time can be redeemed. There are things you learned about God and about humanity in those years of life, things you may not even know you learned. Now is the time to make the whole life you have lived till now a matter of prayer and prayerful reflection. Take those days. Turn them over prayerfully in your heart. Mine them for the wisdom buried there. Open those years to the reflective care of the community of faith too. Invite your people into your prayers and reflections. All of ministry is a spiritual exercise, as is all of life. Those years will become for you, I firmly believe, a rich resource for teaching the congregation you serve. Baxter observes, "We have the depth of God's bottomless love and mercy, the depth of the mystery of His designs . . . and the depth of their own hearts to disclose."[43] There is no way to be true to this ministry, ultimately to disclose the depths of the hearts of our people, if we're not dedicated to disclosing the depths of our own hearts.

Obviously there are dangers in disclosing our hearts, not the least being a sort of spiritual narcissism that sadly affects some of our colleagues. Their incessant self-referencing and navel-gazing gives spirituality a bad name. But I trust that you will not do that, and I encourage you to find colleagues and congregants who will hold you accountable, and will call you on it if you do tend in that direction. I think, on the whole, at least for you, the alternative is the greater temptation, to hide your light under a bushel and therefore to rob your congregation of your experience.

Sincerely,

Dear Mal,

I'm still reeling from what you said last night on the phone. Even though your mom gave me a heads-up before you called, I was not entirely prepared for the details. Last night you asked me a question that I hope I can reflect on more fully now, in the light of day. "Why didn't I see this coming?" It's a really good question. You always seem to ask really good questions. I may have some answers to that question, but to get there I need to think out loud a little.

I have to say that Mr. Grimsby's actions surprise me. I knew he had lobbied the pastor nominating committee pretty hard to get his nephew into the position you now hold. And I thought his sniping and complaining about you would subside as he got to know you. Worst-case scenario? I thought he might leave your congregation. I wasn't prepared for him to do what he did.

I really cannot imagine someone standing in the middle of a Sunday worship service when prayer requests are being made, and under the guise of requesting prayers "for the future of the church" (did I get that right?), reading off a list of "charges" against the pastor. And the charges! "Does not dress appropriately." (Because you wore cutoff jeans and a T-shirt to the youth car wash.) "Is involved in inappropriate sexual activities." (Because you pecked your fiancée on the lips before she got into your parents' car.) "Does not care about the spiritual lives of our children." (I forget why now.) That's everything on the list I can remember. I know he made several more charges.

Of course, it's foolish to get bogged down in the details of the list. As Edwin Friedman always said, focus on the process, not the content! Beyond reminding us that pastors really do live in fishbowls, I'm not sure the details of the "charges" serve much purpose. But the process, the "charging," that's a different story.

I'm sure you're right — most of the congregation had to be flabbergasted. Probably embarrassed too.

This sort of event takes on a life of its own in a congregation. I remember in my first congregation, at the close of the Lord's Supper one Sunday, the senior pastor and I were serving communion to the elders, who were in the front row. He served the bread and I served the cup, and because he was wearing a microphone, every time he said, "This is the body of Christ," you could hear him all over the building. I wasn't miked, so when I said to each elder, "This is the blood of Christ," only the elder and I could hear me. After communion the pastor invited the congregation to share their "celebrations and concerns," a lot like your time of prayer requests, and a woman stood up and said she thought it was shameful that the new associate pastor had such contempt for the sacrifice of Jesus Christ that he wouldn't even utter the words, "This is the blood of Christ." She went on for some time, demanding to know what they teach pastors these days in seminary that makes them deny the saving power of Christ's blood.

The senior pastor, who was at the pulpit throughout her comments, tried to interrupt, but she wouldn't let him. When she finished, he told her as gently as possible that I had said "This is the blood of Christ" to every elder, but that the congregation couldn't hear me because I wasn't wearing a microphone.

She was so embarrassed that she never returned to worship again in that church, and neither did a couple that was visiting our church for the first time.

You said you've made every effort to hear Mr. Grimsby's complaints, and that nothing you said would satisfy him. I really thought you had something of a breakthrough a few weeks ago. You told me the two of you talked in your office that day, and you asked him, "Is there anything I can do, anything I can change about myself, to make me acceptable to you as your pastor?" He answered, "No, I just don't want you to be my pastor. I want you to leave." And you said, "I want to be your pastor. And I'll do anything I can to be a good pastor to you and your family, but I'm not leaving. God has called me to this church." I thought perhaps your frankness and openness might help the relationship. It didn't, but I think you did the right thing by trying.

Years ago a pastor told me that one of the most important things to figure out is whether you have on your hands a problem or a predicament. If it's a problem it has a solution. You face the problem, figure it out, solve it, and move on. But if it's a predicament, you just have to live through it as faithfully as you can. What you have here is a predicament, Malcolm.

Why didn't you see it coming? Maybe there's no way you could have seen it coming. Really. We need to reflect on it, turn it over a few times. We need to make sure that you learn as much as you can from it. But maybe you couldn't have seen this coming.

I know I've warned you before about not seeing what's right in front of you because you wanted so badly to see something else. You reminded me last night when we talked that I had told you several times not to shut your eyes to reality just because it is unpleasant. You even quoted Machiavelli to me, something like, "It is better to face reality than to live in an imaginary world."[44]

Yes, I agree with you, and even with Machiavelli (at least this time). It's better for a pastor to see what's really going on than to be blinded by sentimentality, or wishful thinking, or romantic notions, or utopian ideas about how people should act or what the church ought to be. But I'm not sure you were so much naive this time as simply blindsided. I'd rather have you take the risk you did for the sake of grace than simply play it safe with Mr. Grimsby. Jesus seems to want his followers to hold together the cunning of the serpent with the innocence of the dove. [45]

The more important question today — even more important than figuring out why you didn't see this coming — is what you will do now.

Recently I heard a sermon in which a pastor was talking about Walter Brueggemann's way of looking at the Psalms. He said Brueggemann has three categories of psalms: orientation, disorientation, and reorientation. Lots of people think that is what Brueggemann teaches. In fact, it is not. The categories are orientation, disorientation, and new orientation.[46] The difference between reorientation and new orientation is crucial, and it has a lot to do with how we handle crises as pastors.

There's no going back. There's no reorientation that erases Mr. Grimsby's anger at you or his actions in the worship service. You don't get "the way we were" back. What happened in church Sunday can't be undone. Whatever future you and the church have, whatever future you and Mr. Grimsby have, lies on the other side of this event.

I have counseled married couples who have said and done the most awful things to each other, and who say, "I just want us to be the way we were before." But they can't be the way they were before. Something has happened that cannot be wished away.

When a church experiences this sort of pain, it becomes part of the life of the community. Whatever healing is possible lies on the other side of that event. This is why I'm so ambivalent about the way some people talk about conflict resolution or conflict management, as though the pastor's role is to resolve the conflict and allow the parties to return to their prior relationship or reestablish the status quo. Our task as pastors is to be with persons sometimes in the midst of conflict but always moving forward into God's future, toward the new orientation, the life of wholeness toward which God calls us. I am reminded that the resurrected Jesus bears the scars of the crucifixion. He is not restored to the life he lived before the crucifixion (he is not just resuscitated); he is raised from the dead. And the resurrected body, glorified and whole, shows the tracks of the conflict through which Christ passed.

Now this doesn't give you the right to go around comparing yourself to Jesus, and Mr. Grimsby to those who crucified him. In fact, the church will bear the scars of this conflict, and that includes both you and Mr. Grimsby.

You said you have already heard from several members of your congregation who are concerned about you. Several elders have come by to visit with you about the situation. It sounds to me like they want to show you their support. Of course this is positive. You also said you want to reach out to Mr. Grimsby, to try to reconcile with him.

If you do decide to pay Mr. Grimsby a visit — and I think it's commendable that you want to reach out to him — don't go alone. This is very important. Take a layperson along, perhaps one of the church elders, someone who has an unimpeachable reputation for fairness. You don't want to get into a situation in which Mr. Grimsby gets angry and says later that you came to his house and said something inappropriate to him. Even when you are as innocent as a dove, don't fail to be as prudent as you can be.

You'll probably hear me on the other end of a phone line before this letter reaches you. Just know that my prayers are with you.

Sincerely,

Dear Dorothy,

I'm not sure whether you've noticed what I'm doing in our letters. Maybe I've been too subtle — though subtlety is definitely not my usual problem. Whenever you've asked for advice, or as you put it, "professional advice about pastoral counseling," I've largely avoided phrasing my response in these terms. I want to encourage you to think of the pastor's ministry more broadly.

I know your seminary is one of the leaders in the teaching of pastoral counseling and therapy, and that some of your classmates became professional therapists. But your ministry as a pastor is much broader, and I don't think the language and ethos of the therapeutic professions are necessarily the best sources. Again, this is not because I (in any way) look down on the profession of pastoral counseling. To the contrary, I engaged in private practice as a pastoral counselor several years ago myself. What I want to stress is simply the distinctiveness of the calling to which you are called as a pastor, and the way the pastoral calling may alter your perspective on virtually everything — including pastoral counseling.

For example, in your last letter you remarked that whenever you visit a member of your congregation in the hospital, you always ask for permission to pray. You want to honor the person's freedom not to be prayed for. You also mentioned that when you prayed for Mrs. Rose, you felt that you could not ask God to heal her because you had just learned that she had been diagnosed with inoperable cancer, and that the doctors were not optimistic.

Okay, I understand that you think it's common courtesy to ask your members whether they'd like you to pray for them when they're in the hospital. And I can understand how a hospital chaplain visiting strangers would want to make doubly sure he or she were not transgressing a professional boundary. Many people in the hospital might resent receiving a spiritual or religious service if they were of another faith or of no faith at all. But, really, for the life of me, I cannot imagine why else you visit members of your congregation when they're sick *except* to pray for them. I can't tell you how often I have visited with people in the hospital who were puzzled and dismayed because their minister came by to see them, talked to them, listened to them, then left without praying for them. There *is* a sense in which pastoral ministry is a "helping profession," like nursing and social work. But there's also a sense in which it is something altogether different. Listening is important, and I can't tell you how long it took me to learn the wisdom of the old clinical pastoral education adage, "Don't just do something, stand there!" But I would wager that your people want you to pray for them as much if not more than they want you to listen to them. And what's more, they *need* you to pray for them.

It's possible you're thinking of prayer as a sort of zipper that closes a pastoral visit, instead of as that event from which everything else in the visit flows. I want you to try something. Next time you make a visit, ask your church member shortly after you arrive what he or she needs you to pray for. Listen carefully to what the member tells you. Then gather up these concerns and bring them to God in prayer. Prayer in itself is a crucial ministry. God wants us to pray. God invites us to bring our concerns and fears and disappointments to God's throne of mercy.

I'll wager you that the person you pray for will be ready *after* the prayer to open up at a level of intimacy that will surprise you. Why? Because, with his or her deepest needs and heartfelt concerns on your lips, you will have ushered that person into the very presence of the living God. I can't tell you how often I have prayed at the "end" of a pastoral visit, only to look up at the end of the prayer into the face of the sick person, or into the face of a loved one, and realizing, "*Now* the pastoral conversation is about to start!"

By the way, when you said you "say a prayer," I have to admit I stumbled a bit. Isn't it theologically and spiritually more appropriate to say "I prayed" than "I said a prayer"? Maybe I'm just being picky. I don't know. But I don't look at prayers as recitations. They are real communications, though often formal and sometimes written. When we pray the Psalms, for example, we are really praying!

Your comments about Mrs. Rose bother me on another level, and I might as well get this off my chest too. You said she has been diagnosed with inoperable lung cancer, and that you just don't feel comfortable praying that she will be healed. You imply that it is somehow more spiritual in this case to treat prayer as a process by which she and her family can come to terms with the situation.

My first inclination is to tell you that if my wife ever has cancer again, I won't be asking you for a pastoral visit. Okay, I buy the argument that you don't want to give people false hopes. But why are you giving up on her health without a fight? If my wife has inoperable cancer, the doctor may not be optimistic, but that's his business. The lab technician, the people in the MRI department, even the nurses may not see much reason to hope. But the pastor? I expect him or her to pray for her to get well. Maybe God hasn't given up! I find it strange when pastors (and a lot of other Christians too) believe they have a duty to be more "spiritual" than God — they assume that the really "spiritual" course is not to engage in something so popular, so vulgar, as petitionary or intercessory prayer for a person's physical health. For whatever reason, God blesses prayers of intercession. God invites us to pray for our physical needs.

Certainly, there are all sorts of prayers, and I agree that prayer may take the role of bringing us to accept some things we would rather avoid. Yes, there are times when the function of prayer is to change our minds and hearts, and to bring them into line with God's greater will, even when we cannot understand why God wills certain things. I also accept that God does not answer every prayer the way we might wish. But that doesn't mean we shouldn't ask, even when what we ask flies in the face of medical science.

So, I repeat, Dorothy, if my wife (or one of my children, or anyone I love, for that matter) is ever (God forbid!) stricken with a terrible disease, and the outlook is grim, and you come to visit us in the hospital, either pray for the person to recover or don't come at all. As a pastor, I would always rather face the awful disappointment of weeping with my church members because we prayed for healing that did not come (and you are right to anticipate this disappointment, and the lamentation that will result) than not to bring their desperate longings and hopes for healing to God in the first place. I would just remind you of the crucial role lamentation plays in the Bible.

Lament is inevitably the response of disappointed trust. Lament cries out: "God, we trusted in your promise to save us, and we were not saved! Where were you?"

Think back through the great psalms of lament: "Why, O LORD, do you stand far off? / Why do you hide yourself in times of trouble?" (Ps. 10); "How long, O LORD? Will you forget me forever? / How long will you hide your face from me?" (Ps. 13); "My God, my God, why have you forsaken me? / Why are you so far from helping me, from the words of my groaning?" (Ps. 22). Laments interrogate God. Scream. Beseech. Blame. Beg. Laments demand to know if God's promises hold true when so much else in life slips away. There's such energy, such fury and sorrow in the laments because the people take God's promises so seriously. The depths of our lament correlate directly to how sure we are that God loves us and that God can act on our behalf.

You are right to be cautious. You are wise to hesitate. Your sensitivity to the potential disappointment of your people is commendable. But even given the possibility for disappointment, grief, and heartbreak, not to mention the bitterness your people may feel toward God if they are disappointed, I would always want my pastor to pray for the best possible outcome I can now imagine: *that my loved one would live, and that we would grow old together.* There will be time enough to lament if this prayer is not answered, and time enough to come to terms with another outcome if such is the will of God.

There are lots of important things we do for people when they're sick. We listen to them. We reflect with them. We exercise the pastoral arts of counsel and empathy with them. But most of all we pray with them, and we pray for them. And when we pray for them, we take seriously their fears and hopes. It is, I think, precisely in this way that our pastoral art, as Gregory of Nazianzus once said, "gives wings to the soul."

Sincerely,

Dear Dorothy,

So, you feel like a fraud?

Well, I feel like an insensitive old fool *and* a fraud after reading your last letter.

Here you are, writing me to ask me as a colleague to reflect with you about prayer and empathy, about providing pastoral counseling and loving support to your people. Here you are, just trying to put one foot in front of the other, just soldiering on in pain, slogging it out as a pastor while your marriage tumbles down around your head — and all I can do is dispense advice and (worse!) scold you.

I am so very sorry for my insensitivity, for my ignorance, and for not asking about you and Frank even when I read trouble between the lines. If only I had been more sensitive and empathetic! Going back now and rereading your recent letters, I see the clues you dropped everywhere. I just failed to pick up your trail of tears.

You ask me if I've ever felt like a fraud. Yes, all too often. Right now, in fact. And, no, I'm not just being modest, and I'm definitely not just trying to make you feel better.

Thirty-five years is a long time to be husband and wife. I am so deeply saddened that Frank is, as you said, "calling it quits." And, yes, I can imagine feeling what you call your "sense of fraudulence, sitting soberly with a young couple engaged to be married as they ponder what marriage means" while at that very moment Frank is cleaning out his closets at home. I can imagine how unsettling that is, though I haven't walked down the road you are now on.

I suppose there's not a pastor in the world who (if the pastor's honest with himself or herself) hasn't felt like a fraud and a phony at some time or another. We are human. Ordination does not relieve us of that! This is not a glib excuse. It is a confession pure and simple, though there's little pure and nothing simple about being human. Baxter, in the preface of *The Reformed Pastor,* exhorts lay readers of his book: "Entertain not any unworthy thoughts of your pastors, because we here confess our own sins. . . . You know it is men and not angels that are put by God in the office of Church guides; and you know that we are imperfect men."[47]

You ask me if you should stop providing marriage counseling as a pastor, and if you should stop performing weddings.

Do you really mean that? That's a silly question. Of course you're serious about no longer performing those duties. You feel like a failure. There are plenty of people who would say that because your marriage is ending in divorce, you should stay as far away as possible from marriage and family counseling. There are also people who would say you must leave ordained ministry altogether. But some of the greatest pastors I've ever known were those who drank deeply the cup of failure, and who brought to their ministries all that they learned of their own brokenness, helplessness, failure, and the redemption that meets us when our own resources are spent. What I'm saying is this: I think there is every reason for you to continue in the calling to which you are called, and that includes marriage and family counseling. I do not say this lightly. I would also say that as you continue in this calling, you should make sure you do so in conversation with good, honest colleagues, and with the counsel of your spiritual director, and a good therapist. In these days, you need all the help you can get to deal honestly and deeply with this profound experience of loss. But I also trust that in the end, even this awful experience can bear good fruit for you and your people with God's help.

I recognize that Henri Nouwen's metaphor of the "wounded healer" has been all too often used poorly, and that there are some pastors who are not wounded healers but wounded wounders. Nevertheless, I still believe Nouwen's metaphor is good and true. Sometimes the pastor who is most doubtful about his or her own resources is able to extend the most in care and understanding to others. And the pastor who is most full of his or her own "success" is the last person to provide care to the broken.

The God we love, adore, and serve is not only the God of second chances. The God and Father of our Lord Jesus Christ is the God of seventy-times-seven chances. The grace you have received will be that much more alive to you the next time you listen to a couple who use their "love" to torture and torment one another, the next time you're asked to encourage a person staring down the loneliness and sorrow of losing a friend to death or a spouse to divorce, the next time you stand up in worship to announce: "In the name of Jesus Christ, you are forgiven."

Perhaps I'm saying all this prematurely, philosophizing

when all you want is a friend to listen to you. But let me respond to one more thing in your letter. It's a tone more than any specific thing you say. I'm not even sure I know what prompts me to respond, but here goes: It would be so easy now to be filled with self-doubt, self-pity, self-contempt, and self-blame (and there's plenty of blame to go around in the death of any marriage; it takes two to tango). I pick up threads of all four in your letter. For some people it is even easier to lapse into these self-destructive temptations than to give in to the temptations of hatred, the self-righteous anger that takes no responsibility for one's own actions, and the self-deception that blames every failure on the partner. Would you permit me to remind you of a prayer that I will be praying with my congregations this year at the beginning of Lent?

Gracious and faithful God: We have confidence in your promise that you hate nothing that you have made even when that which you have made fails so miserably to live up to your original intentions for it; and we know that you are more ready to forgive us than we are to accept your forgiveness in gratitude and penitence, though we also know that it is your forgiveness alone that makes it possible for us to confess and return to your side. Place within us new hearts, O God, so that we may remember, and may never again forget: it is our pride alone that makes us feel that any sin of our making could be more powerful than your grace, or that there is anything we can do that can separate us from your love. No one is so utterly alone as when they surround themselves with all they have failed to do. But no one can be entirely alone as long as they remember that the company of the faithful is made up entirely of forgiven sinners. In the name of the Christ in whom we have been raised to new life: Amen.

Recognize it? You should. It's the prayer you wrote for Ash Wednesday last year in reflection on prayers from the *Book of Common Prayer*. You shared it with me in one of the first letters you wrote me.

My prayers are with you. My prayers are also with Frank.

Sincerely,

Dear Susan,

You may well be right. My comments on pluralism and toleration may be a bit theoretical, though I wouldn't want to belittle good theory.

Several years ago I heard an astrophysicist speak in a lecture series at the university. He spoke in defense of theoretical physics. He defined a theory as a model of how reality works. He said no model is perfect, but some models are useful. For example, when he and other scientists at NASA are trying to project the trajectory of a rocket, they don't use Einstein's theory of relativity or quantum physics or chaos or string theory. Even though they know that all those theoretical models explain the universe at its most profound level better than Newtonian physics does, Newton still provides the most useful theory for getting a rocket to the moon and back.

When I apply his reflections to the world of church and theology, it helps me realize that the argument between theory and practice is a red herring. And so, I would argue that when it comes to thorny issues in church and society (and how to account faithfully for pluralism is surely one of the thorniest in our time), sometimes the most practical thing might be a good theory. I think what I'm trying to do as a pastor is to work out a faithful and viable way of describing reality, thus my thoughts on tolerance in the previous letter.

Having said all that, maybe I need to bring the whole thing down to earth a little more, especially in light of your question, "As a pastor, where do I start?"

Here's where I start: I try as hard as I can to extend grace, mercy, hospitality, and respect to other persons. That means that I want to grant others the basic courtesy of hearing them out, and taking them seriously. The Bible reminds us to speak the truth in love — and that's crucial. But we're also bound as Christians to listen for the truth with love. Listening respectfully to others, whether or not we finally agree with them, is as good a first step as I know. Incidentally, I have found that eight times out of ten a tense, potentially conflictual situation can be defused, if not resolved, by simply listening to the perspectives and the concerns of others. This does not necessarily mean agreeing with them. By listening, what you're saying is: "Whether or not I agree with you, I take you seriously. I respect you. I'll listen to what you have to say."

We are, after all, made in the image of God the Father, Son, and Holy Spirit. That means, at least in part, that we reflect and honor God's character by extending the grace of Christ and the love of God's Spirit to others, because to do so is to participate in the eternal life and love that God the Father and Son share in their holy communion. Julian of Norwich spoke passionately about the "courtesy" of our Master, Christ Jesus.[48] We are called also to reflect Christ's courtesy, because that courtesy is none other than the very life of God, that is, the Holy Spirit.

The second step is just as crucial. I assume that the truth of any matter is inevitably larger and more complex than my individual perspective and experience. It is essential for me as a pastor to remember this because I serve in the leadership of a community of faith within the context of a whole society in the midst of God's world. Remember the book *Your God Is Too Small*? When I get to thinking that my faith, my understanding of God, is the final word on all matters of faith, I need to remember that God is much bigger than my conception of God, and that life is much bigger than my experience. I can always afford to learn from others. So I want to listen, not only to communicate empathy, but also to discover a larger perspective, maybe another perspective, maybe even a perspective that contradicts my own, assuming that my little world can use some enlarging.

The way you ask your question suggests that you'd like to know how I go about changing other people's perspectives on this, how I might try to enlarge their views, or get them to be more accepting of people who disagree with them. First off, I'd want to be honest enough with myself to admit that I have little or no control over the behavior or attitudes of others. I want to make sure I take responsibility for my own actions, and that I treat others with respect, but that I do not set out to change them. But that isn't really altogether honest yet, is it? I do want to influence the behavior and attitudes of others. I certainly hope that in word and in deed I can play some role in God's drawing of persons into the life for which God created us. I would like to believe that I can help others act more graciously and generously and be more open and hospitable and tolerant toward others. But even this motive leads me back, by another road, to take responsibility for my own actions. The best, the most effective sermons I will ever preach on "tolerance" are those I preach with my life, by extending respect to people I don't agree with in the congregation and the community and beyond.

How many times have we heard a pastor or Sunday school teacher speak of the importance of grace, and then turn around and contradict everything he or she "taught" by disrespecting a person whose theological or social or political views do not coincide precisely with his or her own? I've done this more often than I care to admit! The sermons we live sometimes make it impossible for people to hear the sermons we speak.

I also sometimes — and I hope appropriately — encourage respect for others and tolerance for different perspectives *subversively* by setting up learning situations that are likely to challenge the assumptions of folks. Now, I would hasten to add that, however subversive I may be, I hope I'm not acting manipulatively, but am extending respect to those I'm trying to teach. Let me give you an example.

Many years ago, in one of my first congregations, I was working with young people to develop a "planned famine." I don't know if you've ever done one of these, but they can be lots of fun, and great educational tools to boot. We had a youth retreat specifically to learn about world hunger and to explore how we as Christians should respond. The father of one of my most active young people took me aside a few weeks before the retreat to say that he was philosophically opposed to what he called my "political agenda." He said that Christian churches have no business mixing faith and social issues, and that if people are starving, that is usually because of poor choices they have made, and that the interventions of "do-gooders" only make matters worse and the poor and hungry more dependent on "handouts."

As the youth and I planned the retreat, it occurred to me that it could be used as more than just an educational event for the young people. I wanted it to touch the lives of their parents too. So I went to this father — we already had a close friendship (he and his wife were godparents of my children) — and I asked him to be one of the teachers for the planned famine retreat. He said he didn't believe in what I was doing in this retreat, and that I should leave him out of it. I told him I still wanted him to be involved, that I wanted him to study the subject carefully, reflect on the issue biblically and theologically, and that if after he had prayerfully and seriously studied the problem of world hunger he still didn't believe that Christians should be involved in this sort of thing, I would respect his views, and would want him to teach precisely that to the youth. He took me up on the bargain.

After weeks of prayerful study, he made his presentation to the young people at the retreat. He had read three books on world hunger and studied the Bible carefully, and with tears in his eyes he told the young people, including his teenage son, that his heart had been changed. He said, "I love my children more than words can possibly say, and I would do anything for them, and it finally hit me as I looked at the pictures of these starving children and read their stories, that as a Christian and a father these children have a claim on me. They belong to God just as surely as my own children do. I'm going to find some way to feed them and care for them."

Sometimes being subversive works. I had confidence that this man's faith was a lot bigger and deeper than even he realized. He felt my respect for him, and he rose to the occasion. I think a lot of people will do that — though, surely, not all.

I remember reading Neil Postman and Charles Weingartner's *Teaching as a Subversive Activity* years ago. It's a classic education text. According to them, one of the most effective ways to teach is to set up environments that stimulate people to learn, often by posing problems.[49] This is essentially what I did with the father. I knew that if he was ever able to make real to himself the suffering of hungry children around the world, this new inbreaking reality would pose such a problem for him that he could not deny it. He was a good, loving, faithful father. Once "world hunger" took on the face of a child, like his own children, he would change his mind and his faith would grow. Do you see what I mean?

I'm eager to know if you think this is "practical" enough, though it is clear to me that whenever I act a particular way "practically," I'm acting on the basis of some sort of theory or model, whether it derives from contemporary research or the wisdom of Christians past. And my actions also have a way of broadening and deepening my "theory." It's a circle really. Practice that has been informed by reflective knowledge of various theoretical models is tested in the crucible of experience, sending us back to reflect more deeply at the theoretical level, leading us to practice again, while on the lookout for new insights and understandings. The practice of faith and ministry is like a dance. Round and round we go, potentially growing wiser as we live and pray and reflect critically on what we are doing.

Sincerely,

Dear Paul,

Please allow me to resist your request. It is tempting (and "tempting" is the right word for it) to do as you ask me — to give you a list of books I think you ought to read. (Actually, I came close to doing that inadvertently in my previous letter.) I say it's tempting, because I think it would be a very bad thing for you to allow me to do this *to* you!

Every year various bookstores, newspapers, and magazines run lists of the best books of the year. Some even advertise themselves as such: "The Best Novels," "The Best Nonfiction," "The Best New Books in Theology." Eugene Peterson's list of suggested books is of course book-length, and could provide the basic core for a theological library. It's all great stuff, and I love to read the books suggested in all these lists. I confess that I love book lists, and there's something in me right now that feels like it will burst if I don't write out a long list of books I think you ought to read. My favorite list, by the way, was compiled years ago by the *New York Times* (I still have a copy of it): a list of novels set on college and university campuses. I've read most of the books listed, and enjoyed many of them very much.

However, when you ask me, "Could you assemble a list of books I should read to be a better preacher?" I feel I must resist, at least a little. Let me suggest an alternative strategy. Instead of getting from me a list of the books I've read — which would be a map of only *my* intellectual meanderings — why not read a few writers that have stimulated *your* thinking, like Eugene Peterson in pastoral studies and Ron Hansen in fiction, and follow their literary leads into the headwaters of their thought to see what has shaped them.

For example, instead of simply following Peterson's list, read his book *Working the Angles,* and notice in the endnotes for each chapter (and there are many excellent endnotes in that book) whom he reads and quotes. You'll find there references to Abraham Heschel, one of the greatest spirits and scholars of the twentieth century; Gerard Manley Hopkins, a poet of unsurpassed depth and force; and Flannery O'Connor, the great Southern writer I've already mentioned to you, as well as Saint Ambrose, Karl Barth, and C. S. Lewis. I think of this approach to reading as mining a vein of ore, following the ribbon of gold that runs through the mountains of literature. As way leads on to way, you can then mine C. S. Lewis, for example, to see how George Macdonald and G. K. Chesterton and even classical writers like Plato, and a whole host of others, shaped his thought, *going further up and deeper in* all the time, following the veins of precious ore wherever they lead through bibliographies and historical sources, letting your understanding grow as you engage the brightest and the best and the most profound minds that shaped the writers you admire.

You see what I'm encouraging you to do, don't you? Now, I don't mind at all sharing a title or two with you, and saying how much I learned from this or that book. Friends should suggest books to one another, and share also the great and important ideas that these books confront them with. But I don't want to rob you of the extraordinary experience of discovering your own relationship with books that will reflect your own interests and experiences, and challenge you and allow you to grow in ways I cannot imagine. I would warn you also against falling into the truly deadly tendency to feel compelled to read the "trendy" book while neglecting the idiosyncratic inclinations and interests of your own heart (C. S. Lewis talks about this temptation in his *Screwtape Letters,* by the way). There is, in other words, a kind of reading not unlike the piety practiced by some of Jesus' Pharisees — reading just to be "seen" by others. The best habits of reading are like the best habits of prayer. We read and pray not for people to be "impressed" with our piety or our trendiness, but because reading and praying are good in themselves, and are sources of communion and joy and nourishment.

Reading, in fact, at its best, is a lot like eating. Sure, you can get into bad habits, and there's junk reading just like there's junk food, full of fat and empty calories, devoid of real nourishment. But if you're really in touch with your mind and heart (and the needs of your congregation), you should trust your mind and heart to tell you what you need in your diet. Sometimes my body tells me I need more fresh vegetables, and I know this because nothing sounds good to me at that moment except a big salad full of Boston lettuce and green peppers and tomatoes and carrots. And sometimes the only thing that sounds good to read is a biography or a current novel or a classical play.

I'm eager to see how your preaching comes to reflect the creative engagement between your faith and practice as a pastor and your imagination as a reader. The best preaching occurs when the preacher's reading naturally (and unostentatiously) suffuses his or her preaching. The best preachers don't throw around literary quotes to impress their hearers (any more than they throw around Greek or Hebrew phrases to remind their people that they can translate the original biblical languages).

But they do recognize that moment when Tolstoy's observation about happy and unhappy families bears on Abraham's sacrifice of Isaac, communicating a story of divinity with the deepest human pathos. There's something of the poet in every great preacher. But poets, like preachers, must develop their own voices if they are to rise from mediocrity to greatness.

In response to your defense of George Herbert's perspective, that the pastor's library is a holy life: touché. I'm especially impressed by the passage you quote from Proust (who was a lover of reading and an astute reader himself): "Reading is on the threshold of the spiritual life; it can introduce us to it: it does not constitute it."[50] You're quite right. Proust *does* underscore Herbert's point quite well, though he also extends the argument in ways that I would assume Herbert would not have contemplated. He said that when we read a book, what might be called the author's "conclusions" are the reader's "incitements." Proust writes: "We feel very strongly that our own wisdom begins where that of the author leaves off, and we would like him to provide us with answers when all he is able to do is provide us with desires. . . . That is the value of reading, and also its inadequacy."[51] It could well be, as you say, that Herbert is simply reminding us that the end of reading does not lie in the reading itself, but in the quality of life we are "incited" to live, that is, a "holy life." Part of the wisdom and spirituality that reading stands on the threshold of has to do with your uniqueness, your human irreplaceability (how you "take" things, and what you do with what you hear and learn), which is grounded in that combination of gifts and experiences with which God has endowed you, and which translates into your ministry. I'm glad you're enjoying De Botton's book on Proust, and are finding it "inciteful" as well as insightful.

Did you get the copy of Tom Long's *Witness of Preaching* I sent you? When you mentioned that you had never read it (I'm still in shock at that!), I knew immediately what you were getting for your birthday.

Happy birthday!

Sincerely,

Dear Paul,

Thanks for taking my refusal with such good humor. You're right. I did spend an entire letter laying out my agenda for what you should read before sending another letter telling you how to read. All under the guise of being nondirective, encouraging you to follow your own instincts. Oh, well, I never promised to be consistent, though I'm a bit surprised at how transparent my manipulation was. You've got to love irony if you're a pastor, and even more so if you're the victim of well-intentioned pastoral care!

Your remarks about the treadmill of demands you face as a pastor, not least of which is the expectation that your preaching will attract and retain church members, is something I'm also painfully aware of. In a society that encourages a church-shopping and church-hopping consumerist mentality, the ties that bind people to their congregations are very weak.

Recently a friend who serves as senior pastor of a large

church in the Pacific Northwest expressed to me almost exactly the concerns you raised. He said that part of him rises to the challenge of competition. He likes the competition-inspired motivation that he and his staff sense. It drives them to put together a church program so attractive that people will want to get out of bed on Sunday mornings, or get out of their houses or away from their offices to attend their church's programs. There's a part of him that "feels a rush" when he thinks his church might tempt people to leave their churches to attend his.

This sense of competition, he argued, might be (at some level) seen as "healthy." After all, it spurs on him and his staff to achieve more and to produce better and better programs. It especially affects their preaching. He paraphrased something one of the great "princes of the pulpit" (Charles Haddon Spurgeon maybe?) once said: *If you kindle a fire in the pulpit, people will come from miles around just to watch it burn.* That's what he tries to do every Sunday — set his pulpit ablaze. He takes considerable pride in crafting sermons that touch the hearts and minds of his people, sermons that travel home with them and to their workplaces and schools.

But many days he feels like he has a tiger by the tail, and that if he lets go the tiger will turn and devour him. He feels shackled to his own popularity as a preacher and wonders whether his preaching has lost something in his desire to "appeal" to people. He confessed, in fact, that sentimentality has often won out over the clear message of the biblical text, and flash and humor and self-serving congratulations of the lifestyles of his people have led him to refashion sermons to be better received, sometimes even at the expense of the gospel.

Reinhold Niebuhr once said, "I'm a preacher, and I love to preach." Niebuhr never stopped being a preacher, and never stopped loving to preach. There was something in his pulpit demeanor that reflected his pride in moving and inspiring and challenging people, in holding them in the palm of his hand as his rhetoric soared. Every great preacher possesses something of this pride and desire to captivate an audience. But every great preacher also knows how dangerous this is. If you live for applause, you'll die by applause. Maybe that applause consists in ever-larger audiences that clamor to hear you and compel you to entertain more than edify. Or growing budgets that flatter you and tempt you to water down your message. Or the slap on the back you so enjoy getting from the CEO of a large corporation who is pleased he's finally found a preacher who can tell a great story and "doesn't meddle too much."

One of my professors in seminary, in a course on the eighth-century prophets of Israel, observed that it is a genuine compliment from the powers and principalities of any age when they try to buy the preacher off, to keep the preacher from speaking the whole truth of the gospel. He said, "You know, there were powers in Judah that would provide a new donkey every year, saddle included, if the prophet would just preach solemnly about our obligations to offer the right sacrifices in the temple, but would avoid mentioning our obligations to do justice and to love mercy, to care for orphans and widows, to walk every day humbly with our God." My professor leaned over the lectern, gave the class a wink, and said, "Donkeys take all sorts of shapes, of course, and you'd be an ass to settle for one when it's the gospel you're called to preach."

Usually there's something more subtle going on, however, than the blatant methods some have employed to silence or control a preacher. Often it's our affection for our people that silences our tongues. Again, Niebuhr observed this. He saw that the razor's edge we walk when we properly love our congregations is especially dangerous because much of the time we must charm people into righteousness. We must come alongside them, and hear the gospel with them, and help them see the new realities the gospel opens up for us all. The language of aspiration, in other words, is more appropriate for the preaching of a pastor than the language of condemnation. James Torrance always used to say that the gospel is written in the indicative rather than the imperative mood, and I've always believed that pastors tend to be more persuasive when they imitate the gospel's approach and preach more in the indicative than in the imperative. As Niebuhr said, "The language of aspiration is always in danger of becoming soft; but it is possible to avoid that pitfall and yet not sink into a habit of cheap scolding."[52]

And of course, to return to the issue my friend from the Northwest was raising, it can simply be our desire to make our churches as attractive as possible, to draw persons into the circle of their fellowship, that undercuts the integrity of the pulpit. It seems to me that numerical growth of a congregation must be the great and wonderful *secondary* consequence of good preaching and worship, Christian education and mission, and not their primary goal. Church growth is not an unintended consequence. It is fervently hoped for. But if it becomes the primary goal, we all too easily sacrifice too much to it.

I hope my preaching is interesting, provocative, challenging, and attractive, as well as faithful to the Word of God. The founder of the Young Life organization once said that it's a sin to bore a kid. I've always felt the same about preaching and the whole congregation. It is a sin to bore a congregation. Preaching should be many things, but if it's true to the gospel of Jesus Christ, it should never be boring.

A few days ago I was going through my library, looking at collections of sermons. I've collected sermon collections for over thirty-five years, everything from Clyde Fant and William Pinson's multivolume *Twenty Centuries of Great Preaching,* and classics by John Donne, Ralph Sockman, George Buttrick, J. Wallace Hamilton, and James S. Stewart, to more recent collections by Frederick Buechner, Lloyd Ogilvie, Peter Gomes, and Barbara Brown Taylor. What I noticed as I scanned the sermons of these and many, many other beloved and respected preachers was what I would describe as their sermons' *fitness.* Their sermons "fit." They fit the biblical text, the contemporary moment, the place, the people who heard and read them. They didn't play to the grandstand while neglecting the dugout. *They fit.*

Wallace Hamilton's bold experiments to reach the un-churched in Florida a generation ago, for example, never under-cut the fitness of his often risky sermons. They were biblically informed, rhetorically bold, prophetically compelling, intellectually inquisitive, and profoundly pertinent to the lives of his people. Not many church growth gurus these days would counsel a Hamilton to preach the kinds of sermons he did in the midst of a South locked into the devil's bargain of Jim Crow laws. Not if he expected to fill the church parking lot on Sunday mornings! But when you read one of his most prophetic sermons, you sense why people came. He spoke from the depths of a seasoned biblical wisdom with profound respect for the human condition. He reasoned with his people, invited them, charmed them, urged them, and summoned them to the Word of God. He paid them the incalculable compliment of taking them and their lives seriously, and spoke a serious word to them.

Much the same can be said of Clarence Jordan, whose power-ful prophetic voice was seasoned with humanity and humor, as well as an astonishing sense of rhetoric. "Effective sermons come from the laboratory," Jordan once said, "not the classroom."[53] But when Jordan slices through a thick biblical text, you can almost smell the rich aroma of the text filling the room like the acid sweet scent of a ripe garden-grown tomato. And you sense the deep fitness of his preaching emerging from his unpretentious, but undeniable, biblical scholarship (Jordan had a Ph.D. in New Testament Greek) and a heart of faith fully engaged in a time and a place in need of God's prophetic Word.

I'm not sure I had realized this until now, but a crucial aspect of the fitness of our preaching is its seriousness. Now, I'm not saying that great preaching cannot also be humorous. But great preaching does not make a clown of the preacher or of the gospel of Jesus Christ. Preaching is foolishness to the Greeks, but it is *serious* foolishness, bearing witness to the power and wisdom of God revealed in the cross of Christ that calls into question human power and wisdom. Great preaching recognizes that something serious is at stake when we step into the pulpit.

A friend sent me a copy of a poem recently. I don't know what inspired him to do that, but the timing was, I think, providential. It was a poem I already knew well and loved. When it arrived, I was leaving to preach at a chapel service in a seminary on the other side of the country. They asked me to preach from a biblical text of my choosing, but they particularly wanted me to reflect on Christian worship. I spent much of my flight rethinking the sermon I had prepared. I ended up rewriting it.

The poem is titled "Churchgoing," and it's written by Philip Larkin. It tells something of a story. The narrator of the poem has wandered into an empty church. He muses on what happens in this building, and wonders what it might be like in some distant, future time when no one uses churches anymore for the purposes they were built for and all have forgotten what those purposes were. He wonders what might happen if someone like him wandered into a long-abandoned church building and tried to figure out what people did in such places. Standing in the midst of "matting and seats and stone, / And little books," the organ and the "tense, musty, unignorable silence, / Brewed God knows how long," the narrator concludes that even an uninformed visitor would discern that the church building was a "serious house on serious earth," and this much, at least, "never can be obsolete, / Since someone will forever be surprising / A hunger in himself to be more serious, / And gravitating with it to this ground, / Which, he once heard, was proper to grow wise in."[54]

Preaching that is fit remembers its serious intent. Something of real consequence hangs in the balance when the preacher mounts the pulpit and stands at the communion table. Perhaps what most hangs in the balance is the preacher's soul. What is it John Donne says in the thirteenth of his Divine Poems? "What if this present were the world's last night? Mark in my heart, O soul, where thou dost dwell." In some sense, every sermon partakes of that strangely apocalyptic, strangely eschatological compulsion to imagine: If this sermon is all that remains in the ledger of my life, and every other word is blotted out, what does my life have to say?

Maybe this all sounds a bit too high blown. But when I step into the pulpit, I want to remember what (or rather, Who) brings me there. This is serious business.

Ah, well, when I start quoting Donne, I know I've flown a bit too high for my own meager abilities.

Sincerely,

Dear Mal,

Actually I think the concerns you are raising are both pragmatic *and* spiritual. You say the decision that you and the personnel committee reached was neither wholly good nor entirely evil, but that it was certainly necessary.

Let's see if I've got the particulars. With your concurrence the church fired a member of your staff whose performance was inadequate, despite many, many attempts by both you and the church to help him improve. His behavior throughout the process was, in your words, inappropriate. He was defensive every time you, as his supervisor, attempted to help him discern his rough edges, and he resisted your attempts to direct him to additional training. After your supervisory conversations with him, he went out into the congregation and appealed to various members' emotions, trying to enlist their support against you and the church board. While you recognize that it was necessary to take the steps that you and the personnel committee and the board took, you and they feel very bad about firing him.

Is that a fair summary of what happened?

I suppose I would be disappointed in you at some level if you didn't feel bad about this. I would hope that you would never take delight in any person's failure, and that your compassion for others would make it difficult to fire a person. But I would also be disappointed in you if you had not possessed the courage to place the interests and needs of the whole congregation first.

Those needs weigh heavily on us as pastors. We are in a peculiar position as church leaders of needing to see the whole, and not just the parts. This doesn't mean we don't care for every member of the congregation individually. It does mean, however, that we must carry a sense of the congregation as a single, whole, living body too, with its own integrity.

This is nothing new, of course. Saint Paul wrestled with this issue, especially in the Corinthian church. I doubt if there's ever been a pastor who has not wrestled with it.

You and the leadership of your congregation made a very difficult decision. You believe you did everything you could to help your staff member to grow and improve, but at some point you simply had to make the decision that he was not going to improve, at least not in his present position. For the sake of the congregation, you took an action that none of you took pleasure in. My hope is that this action will serve as a "wake-up call" for him, that it will help him take stock, and that he will eventually grow because of this whole incident. My hope is that he will find another position better suited to his gifts. My hope is also that you'll be able to find someone to take his place in ministry in your congregation.

You observed, quite accurately, it seems to me, that "judging is a perilous business." Our Lord warns us against it often. But making judgment calls is inseparable from pastoral ministry.

Is this dangerous to your soul? You bet it is!

Is it avoidable? I don't think so.

I don't know if I've told you this before, but every pastor should start every day praying a penitential psalm, and asking for God's forgiveness for the mistakes, missteps, misdeeds, and other misdemeanors that will follow that day. As pastors we run the risk of not taking seriously enough the spiritual dimensions of our many decisions, and the consequences that follow them.

Either that or we find ourselves paralyzed by the fear of making mistakes. A pastor once told me that the only thing that gave him the courage to step out of the door each morning was the assurance that God forgives our sin. Over the years I have become more and more convinced by this view, especially when I reflect on how unclear I am about when I am sinning. There have been so many times — *SO many times* — when I rushed into a situation believing I was bringing salvation and healing, only to realize later that I had wreaked havoc instead. God alone knows our hearts, of course. But God alone knows the heart of life too, the inner truth of motives and consequences. This being the case, I start each day now with a penitential psalm and a prayer: "God, forgive me for those sins I commit knowingly and without knowledge by what I do and what I leave undone."

All that we do is spiritual, you see. Nowhere is this truer than in personnel committee decisions. We wrestle not only with flesh and blood, but with powers and principalities, with spiritual forces in high places.

So, you see, the issue you raised about your own feelings of spiritual exhaustion is not unrelated. You say that you need to "get away from the grind for a while to regain your spiritual sanity," that you need to "have the chance just to worship, without leading worship." And both may be true. It sounds like you need a rest, at any rate. We should never forget that at the root of Christian faith is the biblical idea that each person is a single human being, a body-soul-mind unity. You and I have talked about respecting the need for Sabbath, of resting deeply and regularly as a spiritual discipline. The point I want to reiterate right now is that while you probably do need to get away, take some vacation time, distract yourself, and so forth, this is no substitute for finding in your daily life a healthy rhythm of work and rest, spiritual renewal and giving, breathing in and breathing out. If our respiration consists only in expiring, we'll probably do that before our time, if you get my drift. Don't forget that in the Bible, both in the Hebrew and the Greek, the words for Spirit are also the words for breath.

While we can all benefit from participating in worship we don't lead, don't believe the myth that you can't worship if you're leading it. This is simply not true. Indeed, I would argue that pastors are peculiarly the sorts of people who worship best when they lead worship. Even if I'm overstating the case a bit, it is undoubtedly true that pastors must learn to gain spiritual nourishment from their preparation for preaching and worship and from their actual preaching and leadership of worship *if they are going to be regularly nourished.* It's not a shortcoming in your spiritual life that when you read the Bible, you generally read it with a preacher's eye toward preaching. It's not a shortcoming in your spiritual life that when you lead worship, you do so with a kind of attentiveness to "what comes next" that many of your congregants simply don't possess. Worship is fundamentally a kind of work, a kind of service we owe to an infinitely adorable God. Worship gives life to us even when we lead it bone tired, weary and ragged at the edges, as we sometimes do on the Lord's Day.

You need rest right now — spiritual rest, mental rest, and physical rest — and I want you to make sure you take better care of yourself. You haven't taken a vacation in far too long. But don't blame your exhaustion, even your spiritual exhaustion, on the idea that as a pastor you aren't able to get spiritual nourishment the way your laypeople get it. You aren't a layperson. You're a pastor. And, strangely enough, God has woven into our vocation some wonderful means of receiving daily nourishment, means that do not require us to retire to a retreat center. Every day we can and must pray. Every day we can and should read the Bible. The Psalms are at our elbows, the testimonies of the saints stand on our bookshelves and bedside tables ready to encourage us even in the most difficult of days. Every Sunday Christ is raised again to new life on the Lord's Day, and we are raised with him by the power of God's Spirit. There we stand in the midst of it all, preaching, presiding at the Lord's Table, baptizing, welcoming, sending forth, listening throughout the service beneath the cues on the page of the worship bulletin for the whisper of God's eternal Word and Spirit.

It's not at all uncommon for beginning pastors to feel overwhelmed when leading worship. And it would be just silly of me to tell you that you'll feel nourished on Sundays when, much of the time, you are struggling simply to learn and to remember what you need to do. A beginning musician must learn enough to get beyond "playing the notes" in order to "play the music." But in time, great musicians are fed by the music they play. So it is with pastors and worship.

Can those who lead worship also at the same time worship God? Yes, they can.

In fact, after thirty years of being a pastor, I have to say I worship God much better, much more attentively and actively, when I lead worship than when I attend worship led by others. Week after week I am surprised by how God speaks to me in the midst of the worship I am leading. Though sometimes I leave worship tired, I seldom leave worship empty. As a pastor, my spiritual life is grounded here in the worship of the congregation I lead. And all the other spiritual disciplines I am engaged in, somehow point to the gathering of this congregation with whom I listen to God's Word by preaching.

As I read back over this letter, it occurs to me that I'm giving the impression that the purpose of worship is to nourish us, or "fill us up." Several years ago I remarked to another pastor that I "needed" worship that day because I felt so spiritually empty. He corrected me rather sternly and said that the purpose of worship is not to make me feel better. Worship is an end in itself. The proper end of worship is simply the worship of God. Our nourishment and refreshment are by-products, secondary benefits, not the ultimate goal of our worship. I felt chastened by his remarks, and still feel the sting a little. I think he's basically right, although I would add that these secondary benefits are wonderful, and from a human perspective they matter deeply.

Sincerely,

Dear Jim,

Before I address your comment about "fund-raising" in the church, let me backtrack a little to the comments you made about theological reflection. You said that in the internship you did in seminary your supervising pastor asked you to reflect theologically on your ministry. I'm not sure whether it was the pastor or you who decided that theological reflection meant that you had to discover which "theological doctrine" was at stake in each ministry case study you did, but I find the notion odd. At the very least, doing that is only a start.

To reflect theologically is to explore what it means in any particular situation to understand our lives in relationship to God. What does it mean that we place our trust in the God and Father of our Lord Jesus Christ? What does it mean for us to love and worship and serve this infinitely adorable God? Theological reflection requires us to ask all sorts of questions in this vein in the midst of the lives we live.

For example, a young mother of two children dies suddenly of cancer. Where is God to be found in the midst of this tragedy?

A church becomes conscious of its steady numerical decline. What response by the church and its pastor would most honor and glorify God?

An elderly couple survey their lives, aware that they have been financially blessed beyond their wildest dreams. How can their resources express their gratitude to God and their stewardship of the life God has given them?

Theological reflection represents the persistent and sometimes hard work of discerning God's presence among us, and of making sense of God's apparent absence. It tries to account for God's grace as well as God's law, God's judgment as well as God's mercy. I would say that theological reflection is the ordinary, essential, and indispensable work of the pastor.

Is theological reflection connected somehow to a deep understanding of the church's doctrines? Of course it is.

Is it related to a vital knowledge of the Bible and of the confessions and creeds of our faith heritage? Yes.

But theological reflection is essentially a living and dynamic activity, something we engage in moment to moment. It requires a creative and critical as well as a constructive engagement with the foundations of our faith, and a rational facility as well as an affective willingness to ask tough questions about what we believe and hope. In other words, it is a lot more difficult (and a lot more fun) than simply finding the hidden "doctrine" within a pastoral conversation.

Sometimes, by the way, theological reflection may indeed mean discovering that the crisis in Mr. and Mrs. Broomfield's marriage revolves around an inadequate "doctrine" of the atonement. Mr. Broomfield may never really have been able to believe that God can forgive the inexcusable. And thus his whole way of dealing with himself and his wife and his children and everyone around him may have been to try to "earn" redemption for himself, and to make other people "earn" it too — including the everyday redemption of forgiving and loving other people amid life's ordinary falls and scrapes.

But discovering that the problem is, at root, the doctrine of the atonement is just the bare, minimal, first step toward theological reflection. It leads to all sorts of "theological" questions, like: What happened in Mr. Broomfield's past that has shaped him this way instead of some other way? What's going on in his life now to further that situation? What would it cost him to give up his "salvation by works"? How, as a pastor, do you gain access to his heart and mind so you can help him grow in Christ, and come to realize that grace is precisely the thing that cannot be earned or deserved? How do you help him and his family heal the damage that has been done from decades of living by the sword of "works righteousness," trying to earn God's approval and Mr. Broomfield's? How will this family learn to cope when they begin to grow in spiritual and emotional health? Grace, like discipleship, has its costs. Not all the consequences of grace are pleasant or comfortable, at least not in the short term.

Do you see what I mean? Theological reflection is not a parlor game. It is the core occupation — the core *vocation* — of the pastor, and it holds the promise and threat of taking us deep into the heart of the living God's encounter with humanity — not humanity in abstraction, but *our* humanity.

That said, let's turn to fund-raising in the church — what you asked about in your letter. The issue relates directly to theological reflection — what we've been talking about. I am aware that your principal way of thinking about the leadership of the church derives from years of success in the business world. This is your default setting. And there are times where your business experience may be valuable. But there is a whole invisible culture of assumed values and goals, and a whole vocabulary, that is part of that earlier experience (and representative of the larger society in which we live) that is not only foreign to certain aspects of Christian ministry, but may even be antithetical to it.

Let me cut to the chase. You refer to members of your congregation as "giving units." People are not "giving units"! The people in your congregation are men and women and children. They are persons. Persons made in the image of God. God's creatures. And by God's gracious adoption in Jesus Christ, they are children of God. You're flirting with something very dangerous when you allow your language to reduce the mystery of God's creation to mere economic terms!

The culture at large does the same thing. Human beings — men, women, and children — are regularly reduced to the status of "consumers" in our society. I don't think I'm playing a game of semantics here. I'm trying to be theologically and pastorally responsible and appropriate in my use of language. I'm trying to use the right word, in this case the right theological word.

What is at stake?

Our very humanity is at stake.

And if that's not enough: *the character of God is at stake too*, because *we are created in the image of the triune God!* When we trample underfoot the human image of God, we dishonor God too.

The psalmist asks: "What is man, that thou art mindful of him?" This remains a good question, and any answer that reduces the mystery of God's human creatures risks a betrayal of God's creative will.

There are some spectacularly bad answers to this question, by the way. What is humanity? One college-level textbook describes humanity as essentially a portable plumbing system. I remember another writer who describes humanity as a moral entity devoted to seeking the greatest pleasure for the least expenditure of effort.

Abraham Heschel once observed that in pre-Nazi Germany it was commonly said that "the human body contains a sufficient amount of fat to make seven cakes of soap, enough iron to make a medium-sized nail, a sufficient amount of phosphorus to equip two thousand match-heads, enough sulphur to rid one's self of one's fleas."[55] Heschel then noted a connection between the materialistic reduction of the human being to its merely physical components and the atrocities the Nazis later committed. I think he was right. Reduction of humanity leads to the abolition of humanity, to borrow an image from C. S. Lewis.

We take a very dangerous path when we reduce the mystery and wonder of God's human creatures, even if the signposts on that path are justified as simply "technical shorthand for church fund-raisers," as you call it.

I remember how one of my pastor-mentors, many years ago now, told me that both communism and capitalism have the tendency to reduce our humanity for the sake of their competing economic systems: communism reduces the person to a unit of labor, capitalism to a unit of consumption. Neither comprehends the fullness of our humanity. I'm not sure I appreciated his critique years ago when he first told me this. But when I hear you talk about fund-raising, I get a sense of what is at stake. If the church becomes just another expression of a consumer society, where can we turn to recover our humanity?

A few days ago a pastor told me about an exasperating conversation he had with his next-door neighbor. His neighbor is an executive with a large department store. The neighbor was talking about the decline in earnings over the past few quarters, and about a new advertising program they were working on. He said to the pastor: "I'm sure you know what I mean. After all, we're both in sales. Your goods are just less tangible than mine. We're both looking for new customers all the time."

The pastor said he tried to explain to the man that he wasn't in sales, but to no avail. The pastor told me, "I just kept thinking to myself: 'When I'm praying at the bedside of a dying woman, her family gathered around me in the dark hospital room, I know that's not sales. When I lead the congregation in the worship of God, I'm not trying to sell anybody anything. Bearing witness to the good news of Jesus Christ in conversation with those who have not yet heard that good news is not sales.' But a nagging doubt keeps eating at me. Am I somehow guilty of emptying my people of the dignity God has given them in their creation and redemption by thinking of them as consumers and customers and clients too?" Sometimes it's only in the quietness of our own hearts that we admit that we have subtly fallen into the trap set by our culture.

We seem to have trouble seeing how insipid and pervasive this whole (what should we call it — mercantile? consumer? entrepreneurial?) way of thinking is in our culture. It's the cultural water we swim in, invisible to our eyes but all around us. This cultural attitude (could we call it "the spirit of the present age"?) reduces all aspects of God's creation and human society to things to be bought and sold. Like the powers and principalities, the invisible forces of dominion, that Saint Paul describes, this "spirit" (I wish I had some way to label it simply!) demands to be worshiped. It demands that we submit all other allegiances to it, even our worship of God. Maybe I'm just ranting. But I don't think so.

What am I saying? Am I saying that the church does not need money to do the things it does? No, of course not!

Am I implying that you're unfaithful as a pastor if you put together a savvy capital campaign for your church or make use of various sorts of fund-raising technologies? No, I'm not really saying that either.

But I am saying that Christians have a responsibility to think theologically about the church's life and ministry, about the way we do and say *everything,* because everything we do and say must be done in the name of Jesus Christ, and in a manner consistent with the character of God revealed in him.

Christ is the litmus test of our ministry. And it is so easy, so very easy, to unwittingly pour ourselves into the molds of a culture that believes everything is a commodity and that everyone has a price, rather than to offer a clear alternative to this modern-day bond servitude to mammon.

I'm definitely ranting now. I just hope it's not unhelpful ranting, and that you still want to talk.

In answer to your question regarding the dinner at Mac's place, yes, I'll be there, and I look forward to seeing you there.

Sincerely,

Dear Robert,

What a nice surprise running into you at the conference last week! It's hard to believe that so many years have passed since we were students together. I want to assure you that the concerns you raised have not only been on my mind since we visited, but also have been a matter of daily prayer. Perhaps the Christian teaching that gives me most comfort is the one that reminds us that Christ, who is a stranger to none of our human weaknesses and who knows us better than we know ourselves, prays for us constantly. I say this because I am more convinced with every passing year that I don't know what I need, nor what I should pray for. At the same time, I'm thankful that God invites us to pray, to join our voices with Christ's through his Holy Spirit. When I pray for you, I offer up intercessions that you will come again to faith. And I believe I can pray this with confidence. But I also recognize that the outcome doesn't rest on the fervency or frequency of my prayer, but on God's own prayers for you. I am convinced that the biggest change wrought in prayer is not the one we pray for, but the change in our own hearts and minds when we offer ourselves and our desires to a God whose business is transformation. At any rate, I'm praying for you, as you asked me to do.

I wish we could have talked longer. It struck me afterward that you had opened the door for me during our conversation to share any experiences of doubt or loss of faith I may have had during my life. I missed it totally. How many times it happens that we only realize what we should have said later, when we're a block away (as happened to me this time) or a day away (as more typically happens to me). So, I thought I'd write to tell you about one of my periods of darkness.

But before I do, let me reiterate something I *did* say during our talk. God is not a vending machine, into which we put our coins and receive our selections. Though God is higher than any human thought; greater than any human imagination; holy, awesome, and transcendent; the creator of all that exists; for whom a supernova is a plaything, God is also personal, in a sense none of us can comprehend. Knowledge of God does not, then, lie at the end of a mathematical formula. Nor does faith in God. Both knowledge and faith are grounded in a reality we try to approximate by using the word "relationship." But relationship with God is in its own category. It's somewhat like relationships with other persons, but then it's also very different from such relationships too. I know you know this, and remember it from your own theological studies — at least, I know you know this at the head level. At the level of the human heart it is hard for us to remember, however, because we want the relationship with God to be automatic, always accessible, always discernible, clear and traceable in our thoughts and feelings. However, God is in control of this relationship and uses it as a tool to transform us into the image of Jesus Christ. For this purpose darkness, the feeling of absence, disappointment, humiliation, loneliness, and the sense of unanswered prayer prove to be tools as effective as light, joy, the sense of God's nearness, serendipity, and the ineffable wonder of fellowship at the heart of God's community of faith.

Just because we go through what Saint John of the Cross called "the dark night of the soul," just because we cannot muster faith or climb over the mountainous molehills of nagging doubts, just because we feel like we're alone in the universe, doesn't mean God is not very much in relationship with us at that moment or is not at that very moment working on us to achieve God's purposes in us.

You know this. I know you do. You've known it since we sat in the seminary classroom together. In fact, I suspect you've understood this longer and better than I have. Years ago you talked about what it would be like someday to help Christians deal with these spiritual realities. Did we doubt in those days that we'd experience these struggles ourselves as we also grew in the faith? Pastors, like all Christians, are subject to these realities. In some ways (I am convinced of this!) pastors are even *more* subject to them.

The enervating monotony of certain pastoral duties. The familiarity with holy things. The routine brush with transcendence, whether at the bedside of a dying person, whose hand you hold, praying, as she passes out of this life, or while standing in the pulpit preaching human words in and through which, and often against which, God speaks directly God's own Word to the hearts of the gathered community. These are the realities we face, the struggles we experience. I've known police officers that develop a hard, cynical exterior, a shell to protect them from the terrible tragedies of human violence they see. In much the same way, pastors can develop a callus on their souls that protects them from the heat of the fire of God's holy love. In time the callus can insulate them too much, and they can stop feeling the heat of the refiner's fire. The fire, of course, still burns.

Then sometimes our lack of awareness of God's presence may be just one aspect of God's working with us. God, too, allows absence to make the heart grow fonder. We often forget, however, that the fondness born of absence is also a fondness that comes from an aching or broken heart. If I may say so, Rob, you looked and sounded last week like a soldier who has been too long on duty in a foreign land with only a faded picture to remind him of his beloved wife and family back home. Under the wretchedness of a mind grappling with the meaning of life and doubt over the existence of God, you seemed to be suffering, longing to warm yourself at the fireplace again beside a friend who has been so long away you've begun to wonder if the friend still exists.

I said I was writing to tell you a part of my story, and maybe I've spent too long getting to it. But the things I've told you so far are things I believe deeply because of the deep night through which my soul has passed.

As you may remember, after I graduated from seminary I became pastor of a busy county-seat church, First Church, Abbotstown. It was wonderful and hectic. Those were some of the best years of our lives, my wife and me. We had two small children and a fast-paced life. The congregation was demanding. So were the community responsibilities. Hospital and child welfare boards to serve on, veterans groups and chambers of commerce to speak for. I taught weekly Bible classes for our adults and catechism for the children. I oversaw the Christian education and youth programs. I preached and led worship. I did this for eight years.

Then we moved to the city, to a much larger congregation, and started all over. But this time with a professional and ministry staff. From the outside everything looked perfect. And on the outside everything was fine.

I'll never forget the day. It was a Sunday, right after finishing the second service. I walked into my study, sat down, and was staring at the beautiful stained glass window that graced one end of the room when my wife came in to ask me a question. She never uttered her question. Looking into my face, she sat in silence and just waited for me to speak.

"You know what, Sweetheart," I said. "I don't believe anything anymore. Not anything."

"I know," she answered. "I've known for years."

"Somewhere I've lost my faith. Or my faith lost me. But it's like I'm numb, like someone has injected novocaine into my soul. I'm not sure that I don't believe in God. I'm not even sure there is a God to believe in. It feels like my prayers, if I pray, just bounce off the ceiling."

How does such a thing happen, Rob?

I felt like the foolish pastor John Henry Newman once lampooned whose prayer went something like this: "O God, if there be a God, save my soul, if I have a soul."

I don't know if my spiritual life evaporated because I let myself become a victim of busyness; whether I was distracted by the multitude of good things to be done and neglected the one needful thing. I remember reading the story of Mary and Martha and thinking that I certainly am more a Martha, who spends her time making sure dinner is ready and the house is clean, than a Mary, who sits enraptured at the feet of Jesus listening to his every word.

Maybe, like the nominal Christians Søren Kierkegaard described in the state-sponsored Christendom of his day, I was inoculated, vaccinated with just enough of a dead virus of Christianity that my system was able to ward off the real thing.

Maybe the topsoil of my soul wasn't very deep and the faith that took root there just didn't survive. I've always felt that the parable of the sower is the paradigmatic story of faith.

Maybe I had become so much a part of the sophisticated but skeptical world of ideas that surrounds us — the so-called modern world where what can be "seen" has priority over what can only be "heard" in the gossip of preaching (faith, after all, according to Saint Paul, comes by hearing, not seeing) — that I simply didn't believe because I was relying on my eyes instead of my ears.

I don't know exactly how I got there. And maybe I got there simply because I took God and faith in God for granted, and acted like God is a vending machine. Maybe that's it.

Once I was there, or, more precisely, once I realized where I was, I was miserable. (I love the picture of the prodigal son sitting in the pigpen, "coming to himself"; perhaps we only come to ourselves when the stench wakes us up!)

I had a few weeks of study leave accumulated, so I took them. I signed up for a travel seminar in the University of Durham in northern England. It was a course on Shakespeare's historical plays. I went alone, and I made sure no one knew I was a minister.

I was not prepared for what happened next.

The day I got there, as I unpacked my bags in the dorm room, I heard someone crying. The sound came from outside the room, somewhere down the hall. I went to investigate and found a young woman, a maid, crying on the stairs. I asked her if I might sit down beside her, gave her my handkerchief, and listened as she told me her story. I really can't explain this, but without thinking about it I invited her to pray, and we prayed together. Only later did I realize what had happened. My vocation — God's vocation of me — had reached out and grabbed me, pulled me in, and made me be to others what Christ has been to us (to use George MacLeod's phrase you and I learned in school, and that we often used to quote to each other).

During the next days in the Shakespeare class I was happy as a clam — except for one thing. There was no (I have no other way of saying this, so I'll just say what I thought then) . . . there was no transcendent reference that went beyond our reflections on Shakespeare. Know what I mean? We didn't talk about whether Shakespeare was true beyond whether he got it right at a literary or historical level. The more important point, it seems to me, was whether Shakespeare got it right in the big picture. I wanted to know whether or not what he said about the sins of humanity in *Henry V* (the sins of common soldiers and of kings) is true. But it wasn't that sort of class. And I felt it deeply. I felt the void, the emptiness, what was once called "vanity." Perhaps I was feeling that God-shaped hole at the heart of my humanity that Augustine said only God can fill.

At any rate, later that week we had a day free. I went to the great cathedral in the center of Durham, not as a tourist or a student, but as a supplicant. Bowing to pray, at first I did feel like the pastor Newman described. "God, I don't even know if you exist. But we've really got to talk." That was the fulcrum point on which the whole experience turned. Up till then I was torn and miserable, struggling like a man with a fever fighting the sheets on his bed. After that I began to feel more and more like a child, blindfolded but aware he is at home again, guided by the smells of his mother's kitchen to that most perfect place, the table where we are fed and nourished.

There's a whole subplot to my story that I haven't told you. And I hesitate to do so. Because you might wonder about my sanity.

The reason I chose the travel seminar in Durham was because a tremendous interest had "somehow" been lit in me to study English church history and literature. As way led on to way in the previous several months, I began to read the Venerable

Bede's *History of the English Church*. Ostensibly I read it because it was the first real work of history for the English world, not because it was about the earliest English church and its saints. Reading Bede, however, led me to read other works of Anglo-Saxon church history, and the history of early English saints, and I became fascinated especially with Saint Cuthbert.

While reading the Venerable Bede, I came across a historical scholar who said Bede and his fellow Christians were more naive than we are because they accepted miracles as matters of fact. I stopped dead in my tracks and reread the passage. I asked myself: "Were they, indeed, more naive than we?" Bede didn't seem naive at all. He believed that the invisible God was at work in the world that surrounded him. He was startled and amazed by the things (we would call them miracles) that Christians reported, and he tested what they said, and often believed their witness. But he wasn't naive. My lack of faith began to show cracks, I later discovered, when I realized that Christians have always been as amazed as anyone else at the things God does among us.

I mentioned Saint Cuthbert. I didn't know before I arrived in Durham that Cuthbert and Bede are both buried in Durham Cathedral. As I knelt to pray that day, my lack of faith crumbling all around me, I couldn't help but believe that "the cloud of witnesses" is a fairly active gang of busybodies who may, from time to time, intervene in the lives of those who currently walk the earth. And I'm convinced now that Bede and Cuthbert played a key role in "tricking" me back into faith. The cloud of witnesses, in other words, may not be so much a cloud as an invisible fog of witnesses that surround us all the time. They pray for us, with Christ, as I do for you today.

George Macdonald once said that since faith is God's gift, and we don't produce it for ourselves, we have no room to feel proud if we possess it and others don't. We should be patient and understanding of those who don't have it. After all, it is entirely possible that at some time or another, God may remove faith from us, to teach us something new, and the shoe may be on the other foot then.

I want to leave you with one more thought. This, again, comes from John Henry Newman. He said somewhere that "Great minds need elbow room. . . . And so indeed do lesser minds." Maybe sometimes when God seems to back away from us, leaving us feeling very alone in this vast universe, God is simply giving us a bit of elbow room to rethink where we are and who we are. Somehow that thought comforts me, and makes me all the more grateful for who God is.

Sincerely,

Dear Dorothy,

Hannah Arendt once wrote a fascinating essay titled "What Was Authority?" What you said at the end of your last letter reminds me of her argument. She said authority is really a thing of the past.

She may or may not be right. Certainly James MacGregor Burns is right when he says, "The doctrine of authority came into the modern age devitalized, fragmentized and trivialized."[56]

I don't know of any pastor who can count on being granted the level of authority ministers of previous generations assumed. And I'm not sure that's all bad. But I would also say — and this runs counter to Arendt's claims — that most pastors are granted considerable authority within certain boundaries of expertise by their congregations. This is not always an easy or comfortable or happy burden to bear, especially for beginning pastors of mature years.

The late Will Spong used to tell the story of an experience he had as a supervisor of hospital chaplains in training. It was in the early days of clinical pastoral education. They were trying to figure out how seminary students in clinical training should dress. I know it sounds pretty pedestrian, but it turned out to be a big deal. Looking around the hospital, the supervisors decided that they would dress the student chaplains in white lab coats. Within days the chaplaincy training office was inundated with complaints from nursing and medical staff about the incompetence of their students. The supervisors pulled the student chaplains into the office to try to figure out what had gone wrong. They went through the complaints. "They don't know how to do this!" "They can't do that right!" The complaints were strong and insistent, pointing out every sort of failing you can imagine.

"Of course they don't do these things right," the supervisors thought. "They're students."

That's when they realized the problem. In a hospital, white lab coats serve to convey the internal power structure of the institution and imply clear levels of authority, expertise, and status. Pharmacy technicians might wear short white coats, while thoracic surgeons wore long white coats. The coats worn by the students implied an inappropriate level of authority, expertise, and status. The students were held accountable for a level of knowledge and experience they simply could not have possessed.

Will explained, "We took the lab coats off of them immediately. Dressed them in white shirts and dark ties. Put a name tag on them that clearly stated they were 'Student Chaplains,' and the complaints stopped."

The reality for pastors is similar. When you graduate from seminary and put on the pulpit robe or clerical collar or whatever designates you among your people as "pastor" or "minister," some level of authority will be granted you. And if you're a little older, even if just beginning as a minister, you're likely to be held accountable for possessing the wisdom, experience, and expertise of a more experienced pastor.

I was recently joking with Granger O'Connor, whom you mentioned was in the senior class when you started seminary. Granger, as you probably know, was fifty years old when he graduated from seminary. He had worked in the insurance business for twenty-odd years before even going to seminary. I saw him at a pastors conference. He was leading worship. As he stepped down from the chancel, dressed in his black pulpit robe, his hair silver, I told him he looked like he'd been doing this his whole life. He said, "That's the problem. I look like I have twenty-five years' experience as a pastor. My people forget that I've only got two years of experience as a pastor, just like Chip over there. But Chip looks like he just started because he's baby-faced and twenty-nine. They aren't cutting me much slack."

When I was a young pastor (and I was ordained at the tender age of twenty-five), I was young both in life and in ministry, and people recognized this. To put it bluntly, the members of my first church knew I was ignorant, and they cut me a lot of slack. They saw it as a significant part of their ministry to gently, and sometimes not so gently, instruct their young pastor in the ways of life and ministry. To this day I am grateful for them. They granted me what they felt was an appropriate measure of authority in a limited scope of activities. As years went on, they gave me more and more authority, and the scope of activities in which my authority was accepted also gradually broadened.

You don't really have that luxury. Your congregation has extended you your authority more quickly, and you hold it more tenuously. Some people are in fact likely to invest your position with the authority they would extend to someone with far more experience in ministry, simply because of your age. But you and I both know that life experience doesn't always translate into ministry experience, even if you've been in leadership positions before. And if you goof (and you will!), you're likely to lose more ground than a younger person in ministry might, because we take for granted that younger people will goof some.

You asked me for advice. I'm not sure I have any great wisdom on this. I would say, however, that it's always easier to climb down from a low horse than a high horse. Know what I mean? Let your people know from the beginning that *you know* you are a neophyte even though you look like a veteran. You'll be tempted to trade on the authority they are likely to grant you because of your age. Resist the temptation. Remind them that you have a lot to learn, and that you're eager to learn from them. When you make a mistake, don't be defensive. Embrace the fact that you need to learn, and thank them for being willing to teach you.

What was it G. K. Chesterton said about the angels? They can fly because they take themselves lightly.

Sincerely,

Dear Susan,

I had forgotten that pastoral maxim until you mentioned it in your last letter: *"The interruptions are the ministry."*

I think, on the whole, that this is true.

How many times have I been working away at something in my study when a knock (an unwelcome knock!) came at the door, and when I opened the door, I found myself face-to-face with "my ministry"? However important the work on my desk may have been (and it was frequently important work), the person standing at the door turned out to be issuing God's summons to me.

Your reflection on this maxim, however, is every bit as good as the truth contained in it. You asked yourself (and me by extension): *How can we keep our focus when so much of ministry is response to the needs of others?*

The first thing I would say is simply this: we should make sure we're *responding* and not just *reacting.* Do you know what I mean by this distinction? I first heard about it from a friend who knows a lot about Ed Friedman's version of family systems theory.

Reacting usually indicates that our anxiety chain has gotten yanked. We get emotionally hooked, and we react instinctively, viscerally, without reflection. When I react without reflection, I don't usually end up doing much good. The emotional state of "reactivity" doesn't ordinarily indicate a very good posture for ministry — or life.

My second point is a bit more complex: we may serve God through serving others, but we need to be clear that sometimes serving others means responding to their needs, but not necessarily their desires and their demands. This calls for loads of pastoral discretion, and also for a deep sense of your own pastoral vocation. Some folks may think of you as the head of a sort of ecclesiastical customer service department, and that you're there to ensure that their spiritual journey is free of bumps in the road. However, the goal of the pastoral vocation is to help people mature in the life of Christ. The pilgrimage of faith leads necessarily and inevitably through all sorts of terrain, and the pastor is not doing the people any good by laying out a soft detour when only the steep path builds the muscles and leads to the proper end.

I love the image John Bunyan presents in "The House of the Interpreter." Do you recall that section of *Pilgrim's Progress*? The wise pastor, something like Bunyan's Interpreter, *responds* to the needs of the people, but in a way that elevates the investment of the people in their own spiritual transformation and nurture, and respects the uniqueness of God's dealings with them.

By the way, nothing is too small to be considered a spiritual issue. John Calvin once observed that "in all of life we have our dealings with God."[57] We and all things created belong to God, and God uses all the things God created to transform us into the image of Jesus Christ. The good and faithful pastor works among the most common moments of life with his or her eye on God's eternal purpose for us. This is why it's so easy to miss a moment of eternal significance if we aren't pastorally attuned to the ordinary. A committee assignment can provide a theater for the redemption of a person as surely as a two-week mountaintop retreat.

And last, a word about keeping our focus amid the various demands on our time and energy. I was thinking about this recently on the airplane. The flight attendant reminded us in the safety demonstration that if we are flying with children, and there is an emergency, we should put on our own oxygen masks first, *then* help the children. I remember the first time I heard this, I thought it sounded pretty selfish. Shouldn't you always help the other person first, particularly if the other person is weaker or more vulnerable? No, indeed! Because if you try to help your children before you have a steady flow of oxygen, you may pass out, and both of you will be in trouble!

I know some pastors who are so overwhelmed by interruptions that they never get around to praying, meditating, reflecting, reading the Bible, or attending to their own spiritual lives in any way. It's much wiser to ensure a steady flow of oxygen to our own souls before rushing to attend to the needs of others.

This is how I nuance, then, the old maxim that says that ministry consists of the interruptions. I want to make sure that the interruption at the door really is the ministry I should engage in right now. In other words, some interruptions may not be ministry at the door — they may just be interruptions. The thing I'm doing at my desk may really need to be the thing that claims my attention. There are times when I respond immediately to the interruption; times when I will respond soon, but not now; times when I will respond eventually, but not soon; and times when I won't respond at all.

Is it possible to attend too much to our spiritual needs? Yes, of course, if this means self-indulgence in the guise of spirituality and piety. Dietrich Bonhoeffer especially warned against the danger of the church becoming a self-absorbed kind of piety club that just reinforces the spiritual self-indulgence of its members while leaving their economic and political assumptions unchallenged.[58] But it's also possible to elevate self-neglect to an art form. Some pastors take great pride in neglecting prayer and Bible study, as though they do not require nourishment from God's Word and Spirit. I don't mind telling you, I can't do without nourishment of body, mind, or spirit. I don't think it proves how intelligent or strong I am to neglect well-balanced meals. If I'm not careful about what I eat, eventually I will pay the cost. My grandfather used to say that you can either pay the grocer or you can pay the doctor. The same is true of the nourishment of the spirit.

Today, I have had a particularly strong sense of ministry being at the door in the form of interruptions. Actually, half my interruptions today have been at the door of my e-mail server and telephone, and the other half have been the walk-in variety. I still struggle to figure out how to structure the day so that my best energy goes to the tasks that deserve it. Structures come and structures go, as do good and bad time management models, but I'm more certain of one thing than ever: It's largely our vocation itself that helps us discern between the essential, the important, the good, the bad, and the unnecessary.

Sincerely,

Dear Robert,

I've hesitated in getting back to you because I wanted to think more about your response to my last letter first.

If I understand you correctly, you're saying you simply cannot "represent" God anymore. Your analogy of a salesman who represents a company is a lively one. You say that on Sunday mornings, when you stand up to preach, you feel you must either be dishonest to the people you're speaking to, or to the God whose "party line" you are representing, or to yourself. You say you're tired of repeating comforting platitudes in the face of the world's ills, and that your sermons consist of cold clichés about a God who loves us, despite the evidence to the contrary we see every day on the evening news. But is it not possible that the problem lies more in how we conceive of God and our obligation to God, than in any real deficiency in God?

Recently I was visiting with a group of seminary students. Mac McBride invited me to speak to the students in a class he teaches. They had just finished their first course in New Testament Greek, and about half of them were complaining about having to learn the language to qualify for ordination. My argument has always been that if you're going to preach the Bible, you should be able to read the Bible. You should be able to draw close to the Bible, you might say, which means you need access to the languages in which the Bible was actually written to sense and discern the subtleties in the biblical text and to reflect in an informed way on the various translations and commentaries.

In recent years I've also felt that perhaps an even more important benefit in taking the biblical languages is that it distances us from the Bible. It helps us grasp just a bit of the profound mystery of God's Word when we sense the deep ambiguities in the text. I'll never forget the first time I preached the Lord's Prayer. I worked hard at translating what must surely be the most familiar passage of Christian scripture in the world, one many Christians repeat every day, and I discovered just how slippery the prayer is when you try to render it in English. But I digress.

While I was talking to the students, something new occurred to me about the value of learning the biblical languages, and all careful theological learning as well. I had been reading C. S. Lewis's *Screwtape Letters* (I finally had to buy a new copy of the book, by the way; my old one had completely fallen apart. I just loved it to death), in which he observes the difficulty a young student has when for the first time he must read Homer in Greek for himself. As a child, he may have loved his illustrated *Tales from the Odyssey,* and thrilled to its heroic escapades. Facing page after page of Homer in Greek is another matter. But if the student is ever going to really, deeply love Homer's *Odyssey,* he must move beyond the abridged and illustrated version and engage the text on its own ground. I told the students what Lewis said, and then I connected it to something I have come to believe about our calling to pastoral ministry.

The faith most of us bring to seminary is, at least in comparison to the faith the pastor needs, a child's faith. At the very least, it's not a fully developed, critically examined faith. And however wonderful it is, it won't sustain us as pastors. I told the seminary students that when we get that call in the middle of the night that there's been a terrible accident, and we rush to the hospital and are the first ones on the scene there as the back doors of the ambulance open, and we receive into our arms a mother and father terrified because their child lies helpless on the stretcher, a victim of a car crash — at that moment those parents and that child and the community that will hold them in its prayers need more from us as pastors than any abridged and illustrated version of the faith can give. They need faith tested in the trials of our own lives, *and* faith tested in the crucible of careful, disciplined, critical study and reflection. For most of us, the work of careful, disciplined, critical reflection begins in seminary. But of course, we never finish with it. Never.

I tell you this to remind myself as much as you, my friend, that we never get done subjecting our understanding of God to critical reflection. I know you already know this. Please forgive me for repeating what does not need repeating. I'm not saying that your faith is the abridged and illustrated version of faith and mine is mature. Far from it! In fact, the struggles of doubt you are enduring point, I believe, to the depth and maturity of your faith. None of us matures evenly. Nor are we immune from working through it all again and again just because we've worked through a difficult problem (pastoral, personal, theological, or biblical). Life doesn't work like that. Faith doesn't work like that. We don't work like that.

Could one reason you feel burned out be because you've been taking on a role that does not belong to you? We don't represent God. Jesus Christ represents God, fully, completely, adequately. And, of course, Jesus Christ represents us to God, fully, completely, adequately. Our role is to bear witness to Jesus Christ, not to try to do his job for him. I think there is rest — blessed, gracious, and holy rest — in this reality. When we take on the role of representing God, we get ourselves into some impossible positions. We start to think that we have to defend God, talk the "party line," as you called it, even when all the appearances of the evidence argue against us. That's simply too great a burden to bear. And, frankly, God doesn't need our defense.

William Sloane Coffin once said that most people lose their faith because they misconceive of God as a Father Protector "in charge of all the uncontrolled contingencies" of life. "Each disappointment" they encounter in life, then, diminishes what they can say with confidence about God.[59] If this is true, and I think it's at least partially true, there is a corollary for pastors.

It seems to me that pastors tend to lose their faith at the end of a long road that begins by misinterpreting God as our insurance policy against life's dangers. They then move on either to denying just how dangerous life is in a creation into which God has woven such extraordinary freedom, or to defending a simplistic, one-dimensional understanding of God as though their very lives depended on it. Both routes can lead to loss of faith. The first through the narrow, shuttered lanes of denial, the second along the crowded sidewalks of exhaustion. Both routes appear faithful (sticking up for God through thick and thin!), but both, I think, are grounded in the sin of pride (believing that God depends on us to defend God's reputation).

God does not depend on you, either to defend God's reputation or to hold on to your faith. Jesus Christ, as we are told again and again in Ephesians and in the Epistle to the Hebrews, fully represents God, and has faith in God for us. We can rest in this fact, even when we find this fact impossible to believe for ourselves.

Sincerely,

Dear Jim,

Your response was touching and, frankly, humbling. I don't know why exactly, but I tend to react almost viscerally when you raise certain questions or say things in certain ways. I end up firing off a letter to you, then have second thoughts that should have been first thoughts. I tend to *react* to your questions rather than *respond* to them. I hope you forgive me for my occasional harshness in my letters. I hope there is some truth in what I say, even when I articulate it less diplomatically, and less sensitively, than I should.

I wish you had said more, by the way, about reading *The Wind in the Willows* to your granddaughter. That's one of my favorite books. Do you think it's a deeply spiritual book? I certainly do. The chapter "The Piper at the Gates of Dawn" communicates exactly that sense of the holy that the great theologian Rudolf Otto tried to communicate in his classic book, sadly now neglected, *The Idea of the Holy*. There are points at which C. S. Lewis communicates this same aroma of the holy, in *The Lion, the Witch and the Wardrobe* and in *Till We Have Faces*. I frankly think we Protestants have much to learn about the depths and wonders of the holy. Our people are yearning for precisely the sense that they are standing in wonder in the presence of the God, the awesome God, the holy God, the God beyond all our imaginations and knowledge and experience, the God who really can transform us into the full humanity for which God created us.

When, in *The Wind in the Willows*, Rat and Mole stand in the presence of the divine, they are overwhelmed with awe. They are thunderstruck with fear (there's no other word) and reverence in the presence of sacred goodness, power, and "unutterable love."

Lewis speaks of Aslan the Lion, the Christ, the King, "the Lord of the whole wood," who inspires love. But it's love on the far side of awe and trembling that Aslan inspires, because while he is not safe, he is good. In *Till We Have Faces* Lewis speaks of the appropriately dark corners in the temple where mysteries too deep for human knowledge are honored. He understands that awe is necessary for authentic faith, because nothing else is the appropriate response to the holy God.

Isn't it interesting (and perhaps a little sad) that we honor this mystery, this sense of the holy, especially well in so-called children's literature, but we pastors don't honor it nearly as well when we lead worship? I have been thinking about this especially since your letter arrived this morning. There's a sense in which reverence for the holy lies at the heart of Christian faith, somehow deeper even than our most cherished beliefs and values. Reverence inspires modesty and genuine humility. I am human. I am not God.

I don't mean for an instant that belief in Jesus Christ is anything less than "a matter of life and death," as Flannery O'Connor observed in her foreword to *Wise Blood,* surely one of the most amazing novels ever written. But in this same foreword she also understands the freedom of reverence, the predicament of reverence, when it is God we're dealing with, when we're trying to catch a glimpse of the God revealed in Jesus Christ, "the ragged figure who moves from tree to tree in the back of [our] mind."

I sense the same thing, or something very much like it, when Lewis endows Aslan with the power to appear when and where he wills, even in moments when he may not be particularly welcome. God is God. We are human. Paul Woodruff recently wrote: "Reverence requires us to maintain a modest sense of the difference between human and divine."[60] Somehow, then, the wonder, the joy, the meaning of our humanity is wrapped up in getting right this sense of the distinction between God and humanity, Creator and creature. And somehow the wonder, the joy, the meaning of our humanity is undercut when we begin to think of ourselves as God, or when we empty humanity of its special character of having been created in the image of God.

All of which leads me to what I need to say. I haven't always accorded you the respect you deserve, nor God the reverence God deserves as the one who has called you. My tone has been at times condescending and harsh. God called you into ministry with your own gifts, your own perspective and experience. And sometimes, rather than trying to hear expressed in and through your perspective an articulation of ministry and church, I've rushed to demand that you give up virtually everything in your business background and take on my vocabulary and perspective. You've been patient in hearing me, but I haven't always been patient in listening to you. I hope you will forgive me.

Sometimes it is when we are most anxious that we are most dangerous to others. The flip side of the coin of anxiety is hatred. I am certainly anxious about the importation into Christian ministry of a whole range of cultural norms of consumerism and nationalism. I fear the reduction of faith to a commodity, of persons to mere numbers, of ministry to a business, of God to a possession. And so I've reacted to your questions and statements as though you represent that culture. In truth, you and I are both part of that culture, as are our congregations. There are real tensions between us and the culture we live in. The boundary between the culture and the church is inevitably a semipermeable membrane, not a rock wall.

Certainly, I worry about our society's particular version of individualism and consumerism, and its tendency to reduce church membership to participation in a club or a society of like-minded people. But I am likewise mindful of the way faith is not only something we gain through the community, but also something that requires a certain level of personal response. There is a sense in which individualism has affected the church positively, and perhaps saved us from the equally dangerous entitlement mentality common among the state churches of Europe. Transformation and formation are complementary aspects of the life of faith, and the experience-oriented individualism of our society emphasizes nicely the transformation that has always energized the church's work of forming Christians. You have consistently reminded me of these facts. And I have not consistently thanked you for pointing these things out.

Theological reflection, which I often talk about in letters to you, requires the humility to experiment with new language forms in addition to the forms we inherit in our church's traditions through the great legacy of the ages of the church. And I need to be sensitive to what you mean when you speak. I've said many times that the confessions and doctrines of the church always use the products of culture to express the eternal. I need to actually believe what I have said when I listen to you.

Sincerely,

Dear Jim,

Thank you for your extremely quick reply to my last letter. You are both gracious to forgive me and kind to say that my "roughness of spirit did not detract from certain painful insights" I communicated to you and that you feel sure you need to think about.

I promise in future letters to make every effort to extend to you the respect you deserve, and extend to God the reverence I owe God as your creator and the one who called you into ministry. Isn't it ironic that in protesting against the vulgarities of our culture, I succumbed to one of its most vulgar aspects — the lack of civility we exhibit when we talk to those with whom we disagree?

Karl Weick, in an excellent article on leadership, reported the results of a study of firefighters who specialize in putting out wildfires. He observed that most fatalities occur among two groups: those with less than two years' experience and those with from ten to fifteen years of experience. Obviously the first group tend to die because of a lack of experience. But the casualties among more experienced firefighters surprised me. "The more experienced firefighters are vulnerable," he explains, "because they presume they have seen it all and have less openness to new data."[61] When you're in the midst of a firestorm, it's so easy to think your experience will see you through, and that the fire has nothing new to teach you. But it does.

Joseph Sittler once said, "The older I get, the fewer things I understand."[62] There's a false modesty that says that sort of thing but then goes right on ignoring it. Sittler, however, spoke from a deep and real humility inspired by reverence for God and respect for the status of creaturehood. I pray that the good Lord will deliver me from thinking I have nothing new to learn, because the one thing I do know is this: I will not keep learning unless I recognize that I don't know it all.

A teachable spirit is the essence of discipleship. Maybe we can teach each other.

Sincerely,

Dear Robert,

I am having a very hard time coming to terms with your decision to demit your ordination and to leave pastoral ministry, especially after all your years of faithful service to Jesus Christ and his church. I cannot tell you how deeply this grieves me. I do not believe that this period of struggle over your faith is the end. It's only a necessary part of your pilgrimage with God.

There are dark seasons of the soul, terrible nights when the winds howl and the roof shakes as though riven by a hurricane, but God is in the gale, and the darkness is rife with the sacred presence. God uses even these terrible tools to draw us deeper into the life of faith.

I still remember reading Pascal's *Pensées* with you a million years ago when we were students. Remember how we felt the truth of his words when he said that "any religion that does not say that God is hidden is not true"? It was you who kept repeating Pascal's words: "The heart has its reasons of which reason knows nothing: we know this in countless ways."[63] I personally needed to hear this encouragement from you then because I couldn't rationally prove the necessity of God, I couldn't demand faith of myself. You told me to stop trying to make God an algebraic formula to be proved and to take the leap of faith, to take Pascal's wager seriously, to risk living as though it were all true. I believe — I truly, truly believe — that God takes us into these dark valleys so that God can take us through them to a deeper, richer faith and trust. Neither you nor I can make faith happen. Faith is God's gift.

It occurs to me that I too must trust God. Maybe I must trust God for you. No. No, that's not it. I cannot trust God sufficiently even for myself, much less for someone else. I must trust Jesus Christ to trust God for you, even as I rely on Christ to trust God for me, and to share his trust in God with me. We are, after all, saved by the faith of Christ, and not our own. In the final analysis that's the hope we have, that Christ trusts God sufficiently for us. If Jesus is the pioneer and finisher of our faith, that's just what I shall do: I shall entrust you to Christ.

You wanted me to respond by mail when the package that accompanied your letter arrived. I received it, and will do with it as you asked.

You are in my prayers, friend.

Let's continue this conversation, either by letter, phone, or in person, as you think this through, all right? Please pause before you do anything "official." Let's talk more, please, and let's pray together.

Sincerely,

Dear Mal,

Enclosed is the package I told you about the other night on the phone. It contains two items: a portable communion set and a copy of the "Minister's Edition" of the *Book of Common Worship*.

As I mentioned, my friend Robert Albright is asking the church to allow him to leave pastoral ministry. He believes that he has lost his calling and his faith. He sent me these two items and asked that I give them to a new pastor.

This is, it seems to me, an ambivalent gesture on Robert's part, and I think he knows that. On one hand, he is divesting himself of two very real and very public symbols of his pastoral calling, as though to say he wants nothing more to do with it. On the other hand, he wants to hand them on to a new pastor, in the time-honored tradition, as though to say that ministry still matters to him and he hopes it will continue.

I want you to receive them as gifts, and I hope you'll write Robert a note thanking him for them. His address is enclosed. But, if I may be so bold, I would also ask that you think of them as gifts only on loan to you. Whatever happens in Robert's life and calling from here on, these gifts (and indeed everything we hold precious) are only on loan to us. We all hand this ministry along, as is symbolized by our laying hands on a new ordinand, and someday you may hand Robert's gifts along to another new pastor. But in another sense, I hope and I pray that someday Robert may need them back. I will honor his wishes and, of course, his freedom, but I will also continue to pray that he will again take up the ministry he is laying aside. And I hope I will have to ask you to return these items someday.

Sincerely,

Dear Dorothy,

Your most recent letter reminded me of a passage from the philosopher Epictetus, a Stoic who lived under the reign of the Roman emperor Nero. He said, "Nothing great comes into being all at once." What I would say to you is simply this: Be patient with yourself. Pastoral wisdom does not come quickly — nor does it ever reach perfection!

I have felt this very acutely myself in recent days, as I have reflected on my own lack of sensitivity to a young colleague and my inability to help an old friend.

After reading your letter I pulled my ragged Loeb Library edition of Epictetus from the bookshelf and read his advice to a man who asked him what he should do if his brother refused to be reconciled with him. Epictetus said to him, "If you say to me now, 'I want a fig,' I shall answer, 'That requires time. Let the tree blossom first, then put forth its fruit, and finally let the fruit ripen.'"[64] All the things that truly matter in life take time. If this is true of a humble fig, how much more for a human life?

I think sometimes we expect far too much far too quickly of ourselves as pastors. The character of a good pastor — the instincts, the skills, the perceptions — develops slowly in us as we practice pastoral ministry. The pastoral arts are habits that are brought into being, nurtured, and reinforced by practice. It's not so much that "practice makes *perfect*" as that "practice makes *us*." We're never finished learning and unlearning and learning more. This might be the most important thing we teach our people, and it is something we teach more persuasively by doing than by saying. As a pastor, I teach grace by unlearning the habits of being ungracious and by extending grace to others (grace being the thing no one deserves). I teach forgiveness by unlearning the habits of being petty and small and unyielding and by extending forgiveness to others (forgiving others as though God's forgiveness of me depended on it). I teach love by unlearning the habits of hatred and exclusiveness and the sort of fortress mentality with which I guard myself from the dangers of the cross of Jesus Christ.

I am haunted by the words of Richard Baxter. Years ago I had this passage written in calligraphy and framed for my office. I've forgotten now exactly where he wrote this. "Lastly, take heed to yourselves that you be not unfit for the great employments that you have undertaken." As a pastor is called to instruct others in the mysteries of salvation, the pastor must not remain a "babe in knowledge." Yet I know that babes do not grow up quickly. Indeed, nothing lasting grows up quickly. Only weeds and mushrooms grow fast. No one ever made an oak tree mature by pulling on a sapling. Human beings grow slowly and unevenly, and we need to try to have as much patience with ourselves as God has with us.

I think I know what you're thinking about my advice, Dorothy. A decade after you enter ministry you'll reach retirement age. *You don't have time to mature slowly.* But I pray that you'll give yourself a break. God knew what God was doing when God called you with your gifts, your potentiality, *and* your limitations. The author of Second Timothy encourages the young pastor not to allow anyone to despise him because of his youth. I imagine that Timothy might have even despised himself a little for his youth. But he is asked simply to entrust his youth to the Christ who called him into ministry. Can I give you a similar admonition? Do not allow yourself (or others) to despise your "mature years." Entrust your whole life, including your age, to the Lord who called you into ministry.

Are there things about pastoral ministry you wish you understood more deeply from the inside? Are there things you wish you had learned about being a pastor when you were twenty-five rather than fifty-five? Of course there are. But God called you where you are toward God's own future, and I believe that there is a ministry you are called to perform that no one else can.

Maybe it's not so much ourselves we need to be patient with. Maybe we need to be patient with God too.

Sincerely,

Dear Susan,

I'm not sure I have much wisdom to offer in response to your most recent questions. I've sure made my share of mistakes in this area. I do, however, want to applaud your sensitivity to your family. I wish more pastors had their antennae as attuned as yours are.

It is so hard to come home at the end of the day and not track your house up with the mud of the day's grievances and frustrations. I remember only too well what it did in my home, especially while serving one particular church early on in my ministry. Each day I brought home my various conflicts, frustrations, disputes, and difficulties. The tension at home some nights was so terrible that the rooms of our house seemed almost to have their own atmosphere — a thick, dank atmosphere that made it hard for our family to breathe. And I just kept adding to it. I would drag in remnants of an argument with an elder, the complaints of a church member who was thinking of leaving the congregation, a turf battle between two part-time staff members, the tears and heartbreak of an elderly woman declining in health all alone. As you know only too well, a lot can happen in the day of a busy pastor, much of it laden heavily with emotion. I'd bring it all into our home, bending my wife's ear endlessly, unloading it all on her. Even my children heard it, at least much of it.

My wife and children loved me. They wanted to support me through a tough time. They knew I felt alone in my vocation. They tried their best to be there for me. But the situation got so bad I think they dreaded seeing me.

It all came to a head one year during Advent. I can't remember now what was going on in the church beyond the usual busyness. I do remember that one night I couldn't sleep. Everyone else in the house had gone to bed, and I was sitting in the den watching television — or staring at the television anyway. Frank Capra's classic movie *It's a Wonderful Life* was on. Poor George was coming unglued. He raged at his family, his children cried, and finally his wife told him to stop torturing them. I was stricken to my core. No "Clarence the Angel" visited me. Nothing nearly that dramatic. Just a deep conviction that I could not keep doing to my family what I was doing.

As it happened, a day or so later I was talking to a neighboring pastor. He and I got together periodically over a cup of coffee, mostly to talk about things going on around town. I suppose at that moment he was the closest thing I had to a friend, though we didn't really talk about anything that mattered much. He served another denomination. Maybe that's why I decided to risk sharing with him my concerns about my family. He listened patiently, then he told me about a study about pastors and their children he had just read. Researchers had found that children who had been exposed to the inner workings of the church by their pastor-parents tended to drift away from the church as they grew to adulthood. Children simply do not need to hear — too early in life — the political side of church life, the conflicts and disagreements and so forth. They need to experience church *as children,* in innocence and trust, to know its fundamental power to nurture them. They'll have plenty of opportunities later in life to know the church more fully, including its political aspects. I suddenly realized that my own pain might eventually stand between my children and Christ's church.

My colleague said that after reading this study, he and his wife made a covenant. They would not talk in front of the children about any of the church politics they were experiencing. Also, each day they would share one negative story and one positive story from their day at work — and that's all. She was a public school teacher, so she had her share of stories to tell too, he told me, and there had been nights in their house where they had indulged in a virtual "negativity fest," as he called it, right up to bedtime. All of that stopped. They would each share one nice and one tough story from the day, pray over both, and move on.

He said the first hurdle they had to get over was the habit of unpleasantness they had gotten into. They realized they didn't have a lot to say to each other if they weren't complaining about something at work. So they had to seriously reassess their life together. Which marked the beginning of a new day in their marriage, and in their parenting. Eventually he got into a pastoral support group led by an experienced therapist, and she began a course of study in spiritual direction.

My colleague gave me an incredible gift that day: a way out of a destructive pattern of pastoral behavior that might have irreparably wounded my family. He also invited me to join his pastoral support group. Which I did the very next week. That group became a place for me to separate the helpful criticism I received from the simply destructive. It helped me gain perspective during times of conflict. And it helped me grow in grace. My colleagues reminded me regularly that God's grace is not conditional, that God loves me despite my mistakes. I can own up to my failures, learn from them, and grow, rather than fearfully hide them from others, afraid that if my mistake becomes known God will no longer accept me. Talk about "gifts that keep on giving"!

The reality is that pastoral ministry places us in the midst of some of the most emotional experiences people deal with. We are expected to accompany people through all the major transitions of life: birth, marriage, and death, and through their unexpected emergencies and tragedies of illness and separation. We carry around in us the accumulated emotional residue of all these events *plus* our own emotional struggles. It's unrealistic to believe that our families — especially our spouses — can bear all of this. We need places to sort it all out. And we need these places to be safe places — places where we can be vulnerable and open, and where we can have confidence that our confidences will be kept.

I'm not sure if you have such a group or not, but if not, I encourage you to find one. Once I did, the manse became a home again. The heavy, emotionally toxic atmosphere began to clear, and my family actually wanted to see me at the end of the day.

Another question you raised touches on another aspect of our emotional and spiritual health. You asked me, "How do you hold it together emotionally when preaching the memorial services of your people?"

Talk about emotion! I have often said that if tomorrow God called me to some ministry other than pastoral ministry, there's only one thing I would not miss: burying the people I love. Being a pastor means, at least in part, never being over grief. Know what I mean? There is never a time when I am not, to some degree, mourning some loss.

Let's say a family suffers a loss. Depending on how close they were to the person who died, they'll grieve for a year, sometimes acutely. But the grief will gradually subside during that year, and especially after that year. And then it'll be gone, because the average family won't lose a member every year. In other words, few people are grieving all the time.

But you'll probably bury many people in any given year, and depending on how close to them you are, you'll be grieving their loss. You, simply because of the vast network of close relationships you nurture, will be more or less in a state of grief all the time. It raises the emotional water table, so to speak, and much of the time you may be closer to emotional overload than you know. I think we need to be aware of this, and we need to make sure we find ways of talking through our own grief. Otherwise the grief will sneak into our behavior and words in inappropriate ways. We may find ourselves easily angered, easily anxious, and so forth, when in fact we're dealing deep inside with unresolved sorrow.

But to answer your actual question, there is no foolproof *technique* for "holding it together." When we aren't conscious of our own grief, however, it tends to get in the way of the ministry we're called to offer to the congregation and to the grieving family. I remember a colleague (this was years and years ago, and he has since died) who became so preoccupied by his own grief at a funeral I attended that the entire sermon — indeed, the entire memorial service — was about his relationship to the deceased. The witness to the resurrection of the dead in Jesus Christ was shuffled to the margins of the service. The relationships this person had with the congregation and her family were omitted entirely. In fact, there was no redemptive remembrance of the person who had died at all, except that she had touched the life of the pastor. Grief can make us very narcissistic!

I want to make sure I deal with my grief appropriately so that I can attend to my vocation as pastor. "Have I ever broken down in tears while preaching a funeral sermon?" you ask. Yes. Twice. The first time was at the funeral of a toddler. The second time, not that long ago, was at the funeral of one of my elders. The first time is easy enough to see why. The second time, I had buried four people in two weeks, and was exhausted. I had not been attending to my own grief and sadness — and tiredness. And it all caught up with me as I stood in front of the congregation. I choked up a bit, then stalled out completely.

A pastor I respect a great deal once told me about the most difficult trial he faced as a minister. A young person, a leader in the youth group and close friend of the pastor's own teenage daughter, a boy of sixteen, was killed in a car accident. The pastor had baptized this child, watched him grow and mature, helped him through some very rough times when his parents divorced.

Shocked and emotionally shattered, the pastor sat in his study before the memorial service. He made a deal with himself. When he put on his pulpit robe, he would imagine himself as being clothed in his vocation head to toe. And this vocation would attend to the needs of the people. He would proclaim the resurrection. Care for the grieving. Be present to those who needed their pastor throughout the memorial service, and immediately thereafter. But when the service was over and the reception done and he was back in his study, he would remove the symbol of his vocation and allow himself to break down in tears. He would find some distance between himself and his emotional needs for the sake of clothing himself in the vocation of pastor, preacher, and worship leader, but with the promise that the moment would come when he too could grieve. And that's exactly what he did. He buttoned up his pulpit robe, put on his stole, went out and preached, led worship, held the people in his heart. And after the service and the reception, he retired to his study, took off the robe, and broke down in grief.

There aren't really any tricks to this. We just have to be humanly faithful, and aware. Remember: grief is the price of loving our people. It is a price worth paying. But the bill does come due eventually.

I know there are folks who use Christian doctrine as license not to take grief seriously, as though the promise of the resurrection utterly vanquishes all feelings of loss. I also know there are people who don't seem to take the promise of the resurrection very seriously, so their grief is utterly indistinguishable from the grief of those who have no hope. I believe that Christian faith calls us to take the promise of resurrection seriously, and also to take seriously our grief at the death of those we love. There is such a thing as a morbid denial of grief. And it is no friend of emotional health or Christian faith. As pastors, we can do much through example and word to help others grieve well. We certainly cannot afford to neglect our own emotions as pastors, not if we care about the quality of the ministry we are called to provide.

Sincerely,

Dear Paul,

I think your point is worth further reflection. There are at least two texts the preacher must deal with every Sunday: the biblical text and the living text of the congregation in the context of its society in its historical moment. Preachers have to read and hear *and exegete* the congregation in much the same way they do the Bible. Both kinds of exegeses require prayer, care, respect, and attentiveness to the integrity of biblical and human contexts.

It's funny you should raise this issue just now, because I'm reading a book that, frankly, I should have read years ago: Edgar Schein's *Organizational Culture and Leadership.* Schein was a professor at MIT. I know it seems strange to bring a book on organizational behavior into a conversation about preaching, but Schein may help us with congregational exegesis. I just want to pick up on one of his many insights and apply it to the life of the church.

If we want to read a congregation accurately, we must be able to move from the "artifacts" that lie on the surface, like the congregation's "visible organizational structures and processes," to the congregation's "espoused values," its "strategies, goals, philosophies." Schein calls these its "basic underlying assumptions," the "unconscious, taken-for-granted beliefs, perceptions, thoughts, and feelings," its "ultimate source of values and actions," which actually make up its "nonnegotiables."[65]

To read our congregations correctly, we need to perform a kind of textual archaeology on them. We need to study all their artifacts, everything visible we can lay our hands on — the architecture of the buildings they meet in, the language they use, the newsletters, the way they dress, the legends they tell about the congregation and its heroes, the rituals and ceremonies they observe, and so forth (everything visible!). We have to listen for what the congregation "says" it values and believes in, what it "espouses" about the theology that guides it, the goals it seeks and the ways it justifies seeking these goals.

But what we're really looking for lies deeper still. We want to know the things that our congregation really, fundamentally assumes to be the truth about the world and God, things the congregation cares about so deeply that it doesn't even articulate them.

Sometimes these "basic underlying assumptions" support the espoused values of the congregation. Sometimes they conflict with those espoused values. And sometimes the assumptions conflict with one another.

An old pastor, now among the saints at rest, once told me that the greatest challenge for any preacher is to discover the prescription of the eyeglasses his or her people use when they read the Bible. I think he was getting at something that all pastors need to know, and something Schein can help us learn.

Here's the idea that's been building in me since I began reading Schein. To understand the basic underlying assumptions and values of our congregation, to really have a deep sense of the way they see the world, and of the spectacles they use to read everything, including the Bible, we certainly need to pay attention to all the artifacts we can find, and to the values and beliefs the congregation "officially" espouses, but we must do something more. We must also find ways to allow their deepest assumptions of the world to be revealed. And — this is where the whole thing gets a little unnerving — the best way to find out what is really important to a congregation is to introduce change.[66]

I witnessed this in one of the suburban congregations near here a couple years ago. For ages this congregation, which had reached a plateau in membership of about 250 members, had espoused the value of church growth. When their founding pastor retired, they called a new pastor who took them at their word, and believed that they really did want to grow in membership. Not long after arriving, with the approval of the church's governing board, the pastor took a number of steps to help the congregation grow in new members. Everyone seemed pretty happy with the reorganization of the evangelism and outreach committee, the new signage around the church campus, the expansion of the parking facilities, the expansion of the nursery, and so forth. In fact, everyone seemed fairly satisfied *until* the church actually started growing. Within six months fifty new members had joined. Three months later, another thirty-five came on board. Pretty soon there were scads of new faces in the congregation.

Now, this may sound strange, but at this point the congregation became deeply conflicted. Anxiety spread like crazy, especially among longtime members who began to say that something about the church had been lost. A year later the conflict broke out into open disagreements and angry camps. The pastor and the governing board sat down to reflect on what was going on. What they discovered, as you may have guessed, is that the espoused value of "church growth" was in conflict with a much deeper set of assumptions about the character of the congregation. The stability of the congregation was organized around the sense that every member knew well every other member, and had known every other member for many, many years. They all knew everybody else's extended families, knew their personal histories, and so forth. And this deep level of intimacy was now threatened by the growth in membership — indeed, it had already been eclipsed. Interestingly, the church's growth has again plateaued, this time at 350. The "new" pastor recently announced that he has accepted a call to another church. The congregation was somewhat successful in renegotiating their espoused values and their underlying assumptions, but not by much. What is perhaps more important is that the congregation is now in touch with their underlying assumptions in a way they never were before, and they recognize the distance between these assumptions and the values they espoused about church growth.

The reason I'm telling you all this, especially since we agreed to focus on preaching, is this: the pastor as preacher must never lose sight of what it means to also be the pastor as leader. Indeed, pastors lead from the pulpit.

So, I wonder how this preacher might have helped this particular congregation come to terms with their underlying assumptions, and how preaching itself might have helped the congregation renegotiate these assumptions in relation to their espoused values. I'm certainly not saying that preaching can or even should resolve all the conflicts between and among values. Sometimes preaching should *heighten* tensions rather than prematurely resolve them, and sometimes our values will remain in conflict simply because they are mutually exclusive or competitive with each other. But a preacher skilled in reading the congregational text as well as the biblical text may be able to assist a congregation in testing their underlying assumptions in a way that can expand the congregation's understandings.

Of course, if I had been asked, I would have counseled the new pastor not to make any major changes in the congregation for a year or so. A new pastor needs time to learn what he or she can from the artifacts before seeking to peel back the deeper layers of the congregation's life. If the new pastor had waited to make changes until the congregation had formed a deeper personal bond with him, he and they might have found ways to renegotiate the underlying assumptions of the congregation, reforge the espoused values, and grow in membership without losing the support of those for whom growth (and change) was most difficult.

Sadly, this new pastor fell into a habit of simply blaming his congregation for their "hypocrisy," of saying they wanted to grow when they didn't. And the congregation fell into the habit of blaming their new pastor for not loving them enough to get to know them before he started trying to change them. When I was reading Schein, it occurred to me how we in the church sometimes begin to blame one another even faster than do leaders in the secular world of organizations. Schein's almost clinical flatness in describing organizational behavior reminds us that there's no need to get "personal" about the natural process of resistance to change in the church. When Schein says (and I'll translate his comments to refer specifically to the church) that people will not be able to "hear" the truths that are being revealed about the nature of their congregation and may even lose a sense of identity as members of the congregation because their ideals and their deeply held assumptions have been called into question, I can't help but think that we of all people ought to be able to be more patient, more gracious and generous with ourselves and the members of our congregations, to help them find a way to feel safe enough and secure enough to look deeply into our shared life.[67]

Ed Friedman once said that every person who comes to a counselor makes the same tacit contract with the therapist. The person essentially says: *I want you to help me become healthier, but I will do everything in my power to prevent you from succeeding in this.* Much the same can be said about pastoral ministry, but it's not because people are hypocrites. It's just the way things work. I think it is the preacher's responsibility, at least in part, to keep a pastoral and theological perspective on this resistance to change, even (maybe especially) if he or she is fundamentally in favor of the change. We simply cannot afford to interpret resistance in "us against them" terms, not if our ultimate concern is the spiritual health of our congregations. [68]

The other day a young friend told me that sometimes he wishes he had become a Trappist monk instead of a pastor. I'm sure most pastors have felt this sort of tug — especially when trying to comprehend all the kinds of things they must understand to lead their congregations well in the midst of the societies in which they live. I reminded my young colleague of the admonition of Gregory the Great, who warns that if we who are called to pastoral ministry shrink from our duty to serve our neighbors as preachers and pastors, choosing instead "to withdraw in quietude . . . for meditation," God will judge us "guilty in proportion to the public service" we might have rendered. "Indeed," Gregory writes, "what disposition of mind is revealed in him, who could perform conspicuous public benefit . . . but prefers his own privacy to the benefit of others, seeing that the Only-Begotten of the Supreme Father came forth from the bosom of His Father into our midst, that He might benefit many?"[69] This is why some Christian traditions refer to pastoral ministry as a "secular" calling, rather than a "religious" one.

Sincerely,

Dear Susan,

I'm trying to remember exactly what I said that gave you the impression that I think friendship is harder for pastors than for other people. It's not easier, that's true, but it's not more difficult either. What *is* more difficult for pastors is finding safe places to share their struggles and frustrations.

Ministers often tell me they just don't feel comfortable being vulnerable with certain colleagues. Sometimes they feel least safe with colleagues in their own denomination, especially if these colleagues might play a role in their future calls.

Ministers also tell me they cannot be completely vulnerable with members of their congregations. I think what they're basically saying here is that they don't want to confuse their role as pastor or transgress a boundary that might undermine their calling.

Your comments raise a related question, however, one I've heard pastors respond to in all sorts of ways: "Can a pastor be friends with members of his or her own congregation?"

On the face of it, this is one of those questions you want to answer unequivocally: "Yes, of course. If you can't be friends with members of your congregation, who can you be friends with?" One retired pastor told me that several of his oldest, closest friends come from the congregations he has served over the years. He's gone on vacations with them, named his children after them, and so forth. He said it is simply foolish and arrogant for pastors to pretend that they can't be friends with members of their congregations.

Other pastors tell me something different. While they maintain deep and affectionate relationships with members of their congregations, relationships they refer to as friendships, they try never to lose sight of the larger obligation they have to serve as pastor to and to lead the whole congregation. They work hard to remind themselves of their role as pastors, which means there may be times when the congregation's claim on them has priority over the claims of a particular friend.

I don't want to minimize the tension here, nor to fall off the balance beam one way or the other. Personally I've had extremely good friends who belonged to the churches I served. But even in the best of these friendships, stresses were sometimes brought to bear on the friendship because of my role as pastor. One of my closest friends in one congregation was the clerk of our governing board! Our families were close. Our spouses were close. Our children were close. We vacationed together, and ate together regularly. We were real friends. But I'll never forget the weeks of tension we endured because I could not, as pastor, make a particular decision he wanted me to make. The tension almost bled over into our friendship, until our spouses got together, sat us down, and told us they simply weren't going to allow it! They told us to keep our church responsibilities separate from our friendship (and *their* friendship!).

This sort of tension is not unique to pastors, though. Is it? Lots of friends have to negotiate just such straits.

I do think we have to be particularly careful about doing anything that might invite the charge of favoritism that can emerge in a congregation around friendships with the pastor. We need to take this very seriously. We need to keep a healthy measure of self-criticism in play to make sure our friendships do not lead us to compromise our pastoral responsibilities for the whole congregation. The congregation needs us to be its pastor, and we simply must not compromise that calling. But I cannot imagine life as a pastor without real friendships among the people with whom I serve Christ.

We might need to think more carefully about the specific sorts of boundaries to establish in these friendships, however.

Are there areas of personal life we might not want to explore with a friend who is a member of the congregation? Yes, certainly!

Are there times of personal need when we might turn for

help or counsel to another kind of friend — a family friend, a colleague in ministry — rather than to a friend in the congregation? Without a doubt!

Are there times when our pastoral leadership of the congregation as a whole will demand more reticence toward a particular congregational friend than we would ordinarily prefer? Undeniably.

But can't all these difficulties be negotiated? Again, yes! I believe they can.

There was a time when I did not believe a pastor could be friends with members of the congregation. Life and love and the community of our Lord have changed my mind on that.

The great philosophers of antiquity held up friendship as one of the greatest goods of human life. To be friends with another person, to love the person for his or her own sake, was a treasure above treasures. How much more is this true for Christians! To be friends in Christ, to love your friends because of the Christlike virtues you find in them, to take joy in your friends for their own sake and not for anything that friendship can bring you — it would be a tragedy as a pastor to miss out on all this with the people of your congregation. But if we respect our pastoral calling as much as we do friendship, we must also take care not to betray the one for the sake of the other. There's no reason we should, since the Christ who calls us into pastoral ministry is the same Christ who calls us into fellowship with one another.

One word of warning, however. A couple years ago a pastor came by my office in tears. She had become close, dear friends with a member of her congregation. She had come to trust her friend absolutely and had begun to share with her all sorts of frustrations she felt with other members of the congregation.

Sadly, her friend proved untrustworthy. Her friend, in fact, repeated her disparaging words about other members of the church to a variety of people, and the pastor found herself humiliated among her people. I'm not sure she will ever fully get over this betrayal, or find a way to trust again, though I hope she does. But I also hope her trust is leavened with more discretion next time.

Sincerely,

[on a postcard]

Dear Robert,

I can't tell you how pleased I was to receive your letter this morning. I owe Malcolm a letter and will be writing him today. I'll plan to meet you at your house when you return from the retreat center.

Sincerely,

Dear Malcolm,

In your last letter you asked me the question, "Is it all worth it?" as you reflected on the difficulties you've faced in your first year of ministry.

Is it all worth it?

I've asked myself that question too.

I asked it when, about seven years into pastoral ministry, I looked up one day to discover that somewhere along the way I had lost my sense of wonder and joy at the task of ministry. Wrapped up in preparing for meetings, running from one pastoral visit to another, rushing from half-digested biblical study to the sermons I preached each week, being on the road far too much, seeing my family only in snatches between a County Child Welfare Board meeting and a talk at the Rotary Club, I had misplaced the purpose, the mission of it all. I had also misplaced much of the joy I had taken for granted in life.

The treadmill of good intentions has exhausted many earnest young pastors. I was almost consumed by all the activities and the quest for new and better ministerial and management techniques. There's a desperate sort of tyranny we can become subject to, especially when we're ambitious about ministry. One day I looked around and realized that it had been ages since I had just sat down to listen to a piece of music because I loved the sound of it. Or held my wife and kids just to enjoy their embrace. Or listened to the conversation of an elderly person in the rest home just to hear the stories. Or read a passage of Scripture simply to listen for the living voice of the Word of God.

I also asked whether it was all worth it years later when God placed me in a congregation where the people wouldn't love me no matter how hard I tried to win their affection. It felt like a curse at first. But in reality it was a blessing. I had to discover deep down the meaning of God's call as the motivation for ministry, rather than relying on the motivation of being well liked by the people. It took time, and tears, but eventually I came to see, as John Calvin knew long ago, that it is God's call that sustains us as pastors. Nothing less can.

Is it all worth it? I suppose we ask ourselves the question at difficult times in our ministry. Like when we feel truly alone. Or when even those closest to us can't feel what we feel when we bear the burden of the Word of God. Or when being a leader leads us into moments of solitude that make us make choices we know are irrevocable. Or when the daily walk of public faith feels like struggling up a mountainside 12,000 feet above sea level, just putting one weary foot in front of the other.

It's worth it all if we're called to it, and if we're able in the midst of it all to allow ourselves to be sustained by God and by the community we serve. Ministry requires, I believe, a supreme act of vulnerability, of laying ourselves and our hopes, our faith and our dreams open to be known and negotiated among God's people under the leadership of God's Word and Spirit.

Yes, it is worth it. At least it has been for me.

I know of no other life that would have taken so much from me nor given me so much in return. When Christ called me to follow him in this way, as a minister of the gospel, as a preacher and a pastor, I had no idea what lay in store. I get choked up when I think about it — even as I write these words — but I'm sure I've met God again and again through the faces of the people I've served. And God has redeemed me through allowing me to serve them.

For some reason, Malcolm, your question reminds me of the martyrdom of Polycarp. Remember him? That venerable old Christian was arrested by the Romans and brought to the stadium where he was to be thrown to the wild beasts. The Roman governor, taking pity on the old man, told him that if he would swear by the fortune of Caesar and reproach Christ, he would be set free. Polycarp answered, "Eighty-six years have I served Christ, and he never did me any injury: How then can I blaspheme my King and my Savior?"

Reading the ancient account of Polycarp's martyrdom, I am struck by his simple courage of faith (which is never all that simple!). It is a courage that seems somehow strangely unheroic. Polycarp is not puffed up. He is not arrogant or self-righteous. He is not proud of his own heroism. He is not bragging about his faithfulness. He simply seems to be living to the very end the way of the cross into which he was baptized. This surely is a metaphor for the pastoral calling.

Is it all worth it? In almost forty years of serving as a pastor, I have found Jesus Christ to be what my grandfather always called him — "the Good Lord." Christ has made this calling "worth it all." I pray you will be able to say the same thing forty years from now.

The pastoral calling is a lot like certain other callings — the calling of marriage, for example. There are days when passion makes it easy to be in love, and there are days when love is a matter of just putting one foot in front of the other. There are days when love is a parade, days when it is a walk in the park, and days when you just stand around wondering where you're going. We bear one another's burdens in marriage, in sickness and in health, in scarcity and in plenty, but more often we bear one another's annoying habits. Looking back over a long and loving marriage, I have such a sense of gratitude for the opportunity to love and to be loved, to be known and to know another person well and deeply. There's also an enduring sense of mystery wrapped up in the vocation of marriage; despite how much we have loved and how much we think we have known the other, the other remains truly other, almost wholly other, another shrouded in mystery. There is also, and perhaps most importantly, a sense that marriage represents a particular way of being human, and that this way of being human in relationship with another person is itself a means of salvation by grace through faith. For we were created in the image of the triune God, and we are restless until we find our rest in the communion for which we were created. Surely one form of that communion is mediated in the vocation of marriage. That surely is worth all sorts of difficulties!

This vocation of pastoral ministry is worth all sorts of difficulties, too. But no one can give us that which we can only gain by living through the difficulties of our vocation. Another extraordinary early saint of the church comes to mind when I reflect on your question (and I am so grateful that you invited me to reflect on your question). I am reminded of Irenaeus. Long ago he said that when we obey Christ, "we do always learn that there is so great a God, and that it is God who by God's own power has established, and selected, and adorned, and contains all things; and among the all things, both ourselves and this our world."[70] Which is another way of saying that it is in God that we live and move and have our being: and maybe for those of us who are called to pastoral ministry, it is the calling that awakens us to this deepest of realities.

If we were created for the communion that God *is* as Trinity (and I believe we were created precisely to enjoy this communion with others and with God), then surely the calling of the pastor to serve and lead the community of God's people mediates the way of grace, if not uniquely, then at least definitively and fully for those who are called to this peculiar vocation. Dorothy Day once observed that a "saint is a person whose life would not make sense if God did not exist."[71] For those who are called to pastoral ministry, it is only the all-encompassing existence of God that makes sense of our lives. That, at least, is something we share with all the saints.

I'm writing you today, incidentally, not only in answer to your question, but to ask you to return something I sent you not too long ago. My friend, Robert, whom we persuaded to go on retreat for a month before making his final decision about demitting his ordination, has written me. He is returning from his retreat. He will return to pastoral ministry. So he needs back the portable communion set and the *Book of Common Worship* he gave you. Please send them to me so I can return them to him.

Looks like Robert has also answered the question you asked in your last letter. Is it all worth it?

Looks like he said yes.

Sincerely yours,

Endnotes

NOTES TO THE INTRODUCTION

1. Brian Williams's excellent essay, "Mentoring for Pastoral Formation: Gregory of Nazianzus and the Flight of Pastors," *Crux: A Quarterly Journal of Christian Thought and Opinion Published by Regent College* 40, no. 2 (June 2004): 2-9, is a recent example of the continuing relevance of Gregory's thought, and the book coauthored by Brian Williams and Phil Reilly, *The Potter's Rib: Mentoring for Pastoral Formation* (London: Regent College, 2004), makes use of many of the classical sources in providing a theological ground to supervised practice of ministry for seminary students.
2. Flannery O'Connor, *The Habit of Being*, ed. Sally Fitzgerald (New York: Farrar, Straus and Giroux, 1979).
3. Phillips Brooks, *Lectures on Preaching* (London: H. R. Allenson, 1878), 10.

NOTES TO THE LETTERS

1. David Wood, "'The Best Life': Eugene Peterson on Pastoral Ministry," *Christian Century* 119, no. 6 (2002): 18-25.
2. Richard Lischer, *Open Secrets: A Spiritual Journey through a Country Church* (New York: Doubleday, 2001), 232.
3. Lischer, *Open Secrets*, 232.

4. Reinhold Niebuhr, *Leaves from the Notebook of a Tamed Cynic* (New York: Harper, 1929), 173-74.

5. John Chrysostom, *On the Priesthood,* trans. Graham Neville (Crestwood, N.Y.: St. Vladimir's Seminary Press, 1984), 80.

6. Robert Frost, "Kitty Hawk," in *The Poetry of Robert Frost,* ed. Edward Connery Lathem (New York: Holt, Rinehart and Winston, 1969), 435.

7. Gregory of Nazianzus, "In Defense of His Flight to Pontus," in *The Nicene and Post-Nicene Fathers,* ed. Philip Schaff and Henry Wace, 2nd ser. (reprint, Grand Rapids: Eerdmans, 1983), 7:214.

8. Thomas à Kempis, *The Imitation of Christ,* trans. Leo Sherley-Price (London: Penguin Books, 1952), 39.

9. Ronald Ferguson, *George MacLeod: Founder of the Iona Community* (London: Collins, 1990), 290.

10. C. S. Lewis, *Letters to Malcolm: Chiefly on Prayer* (London, 1964; Fontana edition, 1966), 12.

11. C. S. Lewis, *The Screwtape Letters* (London: Geoffrey Bles, 1942), 126; and C. S. Lewis, *Mere Christianity* (London, 1942, 1943, 1944; Fontana edition, 1955), 9-12.

12. James B. Torrance, "The Ministry of Reconciliation Today: The Realism of Grace," in *Incarnational Ministry: The Presence of Christ in Church, Society, and Family,* ed. Christian D. Kettler and Todd H. Speidell (Colorado Springs: Helmers and Howard, 1990), 131.

13. Abraham Heschel, *The Prophets* (New York: Harper and Row, 1962), 2:198.

14. Paul Sherer, *The Word God Sent* (New York: Harper and Row, 1965), 19.

15. Barbara Brown Taylor, *The Preaching Life* (Cambridge, Mass.: Cowley, 1993), 52.

16. Phillips Brooks, *Lectures on Preaching* (London: H. R. Allenson, 1877), 21.

17. Annie Dillard, "An Expedition to the Pole," in *Teaching a Stone to Talk: Expeditions and Encounters* (New York: Harper and Row, 1982), 40.

18. Abraham Heschel, *The Sabbath* (New York: Farrar, Straus and Giroux, 1951), 20-21, 75.

19. John Chrysostom, *On Wealth and Poverty*, trans. Catharine P. Roth (Crestwood, N.Y.: St. Vladimir's Seminary Press, 1999), 7-38.

20. Gregory of Nazianzus, "In Defense of His Flight to Pontus," 7:208.

21. I am indebted to Eugene Peterson's reflection here from a lecture he gave at Austin Presbyterian Theological Seminary several years ago. Peterson remarked that most of the techniques needed for pastoral ministry can be learned on a rainy afternoon; the really difficult part of being a pastor has to be learned and relearned every day.

22. Joseph Sittler, *Gravity and Grace: Reflections and Provocations,* ed. Linda-Marie Delloff (Minneapolis: Augsburg, 1986), 83.

23. Basil of Caesarea, "On the Spirit," in *Nicene and Post-Nicene Fathers,* ed. Philip Schaff and Henry Wace, 2nd ser. (reprint, Grand Rapids: Eerdmans, 1983), 8:48-50.

24. Jim Wallis, *The Soul of Politics: Beyond "Religious Right" and "Secular Left"* (San Diego: Harcourt Brace, Harvest Books, 1995), xvi.

25. Reinhold Niebuhr, *Moral Man and Immoral Society* (New York: Scribner, 1932), 1, 4.

26. Michael Dirda, "As I Live and Read: One Book Lover's Plea for a Literati Nation," *Washington Post National Weekly Edition,* August 2-8, 2004, 23.

27. Alain De Botton, *How Proust Can Change Your Life* (New York: Vintage, 1998), 174.

28. Karl Barth, *The Epistle to the Romans,* English trans. (New York: Oxford University Press, 1933), 28-31.

29. Jeremy S. Begbie, *Theology, Music, and Time* (Cambridge: Cambridge University Press, 2000); Calvin R. Stapert, *My Only Comfort: Death, Deliverance, and Discipleship in the Music of Bach* (Grand Rapids: Eerdmans, 2000); and Julian Johnson, *Who Needs Classical Music? Cultural Choice and Musical Value* (New York: Oxford University Press, 2002).

30. Sittler, *Gravity and Grace,* 93-94.

31. Martin Luther, quoted in Denham Grierson, *Transforming a People of God* (Melbourne: Joint Board of Christian Education, 1984), 127.

32. George Herbert, *The Country Parson; The Temple,* ed. John N. Wall, Jr. (New York: Paulist, 1981), 104.

33. Henry Hardy, "Reflection," *Insights: The Faculty Journal of Austin Seminary* 118, no. 1 (Fall 2002): 21.

34. Bernard Williams, "Toleration, an Impossible Virtue?" in *Toleration: An Elusive Virtue,* ed. David Heyd (Princeton: Princeton University Press, 1996), 18.

35. G. K. Chesterton, *Orthodoxy* (London: John Lane, the Bodley Head, 1908), 83.

36. Marjory Zoet Bankson, *The Call to the Soul: Six Stages of Spiritual Development* (Philadelphia: Innisfree Press, 1999), 19.

37. Arthur W. Robinson, *The Personal Life of the Clergy* (London: Longmans, Green, and Co., 1912), 24.

38. Robinson, *Personal Life,* 25.

39. Robinson, *Personal Life,* 27.

40. John Updike, *Hugging the Shore: Essays and Criticism* (New York: Knopf, 1983), 832-33.

41. Richard Baxter, *The Reformed Pastor,* ed. John T. Wilkinson, 2nd ed. (London: Epworth Press, 1950), 74. Baxter's guide to the pastoral office was originally published in 1656.

42. Helmut Thielicke, *A Little Exercise for Young Theologians,* introduction by Martin E. Marty (Grand Rapids: Eerdmans, 1962), 33.

43. Baxter, *The Reformed Pastor,* 75.

44. Niccolò Machiavelli, *The Prince,* ed. Peter Bondanella, trans. Peter Bondanella and Mark Musa (Oxford: Oxford University Press, 1984), 52. The quote actually reads: "It seemed more suitable to me to search after the effectual truth of the matter rather than its imagined one. . . ."

45. "See, I am sending you out like sheep into the midst of wolves; so be wise as serpents and innocent as doves" (Matt. 10:16).

46. Walter Brueggemann, *The Message of the Psalms* (Minneapolis: Augsburg, 1984), 15-23.

47. Baxter, *The Reformed Pastor,* 65.

48. Julian of Norwich, *Revelations of Divine Love,* trans. Clifton Wolters (London: Penguin Books, 1966), note especially chaps. 2-15.

49. Neil Postman and Charles Weingartner, *Teaching as a Subversive Activity* (New York: Delacorte Press, 1969), 35-37.

50. De Botton, *How Proust,* 180.

51. De Botton, *How Proust,* 179-80.

52. Niebuhr, *Leaves from the Notebook,* 92.

53. Clarence Jordan, *Sermon on the Mount* (Valley Forge, Pa.: Judson, 1952), 101.

54. Philip Larkin, *Collected Poems* (London: Faber and Faber, 2003), 58-59.

55. Abraham Heschel, *Between God and Man: An Interpretation of Judaism,* ed. Fritz A. Rothschild (New York: Free Press, 1959), 233-34.

56. James MacGregor Burns, *Leadership* (New York: Harper and Row, 1978), 25.

57. John Calvin, *On God and Political Duty,* ed. John T. McNeill, rev. ed. (Indianapolis: Bobbs-Merrill, 1956), vii.

58. See particularly Dietrich Bonhoeffer, *Spiritual Care,* trans. Jay C. Rochelle (Minneapolis: Fortress, 1985), 7-27; and Dietrich Bonhoeffer, *Life Together: Prayerbook of the Bible,* trans. Daniel W. Bloesch and James H. Burtness (Minneapolis: Fortress, 1996), 35-45.

59. William Sloane Coffin, *Credo* (Louisville: Westminster/John Knox, 2004), 16.

60. Paul Woodruff, *Reverence: Renewing a Forgotten Virtue* (New York: Oxford University Press, 2001), 17-18.

61. Karl E. Weick, "Fighting Fires in Educational Administration," *Educational Administration Quarterly* 32, no. 4 (October 1996): 569-70.

62. Sittler, *Gravity and Grace,* 124.

63. Blaise Pascal, *Pensées,* trans. A. J. Krailsheimer (London: Penguin Books, 1966, 1995), 74, 127.

64. Epictetus, *The Discourses as Reported by Arrian, The Manual, and Fragments,* trans. W. A. Oldfather (Cambridge: Harvard University Press, 1925, 1995), 1:109.

65. Edgar H. Schein, *Organizational Culture and Leadership,* 2nd ed. (San Francisco: Jossey-Bass, 1992), 16-17.

66. Schein, *Organizational Culture and Leadership,* 30.

67. Schein, *Organizational Culture and Leadership,* 196.

68. In addition to Schein's research and Edwin Friedman's family systems theory, the work of Paul Hersey and Kenneth H. Blanchard, "The Management of Change," in *Organizational Change and Development,* ed. Henry L. Tosi and W. Clay Hamner, rev. ed. (Chicago: St. Clair Press, 1978); John P. Kotter, "Leading Change: Why Transformation Efforts Fail," *Harvard Business Review,* March-April 1995, 59-67; and most significantly, Ronald A. Heifetz, *Leadership without Easy Answers* (Cambridge: Harvard University Press, 1994), has informed this letter.

69. Gregory the Great, *Pastoral Care,* trans. Henry Davis, S.J. (New York: Newman Press, 1978), 31.

70. Irenaeus, *Against Heresies* 5, in *The Ante-Nicene Fathers,* ed. Alexander Roberts and James Donaldson (reprint, Grand Rapids: Eerdmans, 1981), 1:526-27.

71. Paul Elie, *The Life You Save May Be Your Own: An American Pilgrimage* (New York: Farrar, Straus and Giroux, 2003), 465.

A Library for New Pastors

The following book list is not intended to be exhaustive, but only suggestive. It provides some essential resources for new pastors as they seek to understand theologically the vocation of pastoral ministry. My hope is that readers will use this list, as I suggest in the letters, to enter into a rich conversation that always leads us higher up and deeper in.

Ammerman, Nancy T., Jackson W. Carroll, Carl S. Dudley, and William McKinney. *Studying Congregations: A New Handbook*. Nashville: Abingdon, 1998.

Anderson, Ray S. *The Soul of Ministry: Forming Leaders for God's People*. Louisville: Westminster/John Knox, 1997.

Bartlett, David L. *Ministry in the New Testament*. Minneapolis: Fortress, 1993.

Basil of Caesarea. *On the Holy Spirit*. Translated by David Anderson. Crestwood, N.Y.: St. Vladimir's Seminary Press, 1997.

Baxter, Richard. *The Reformed Pastor*. Edited by John T. Wilkinson. 2nd ed. London: Epworth Press, 1950.

Beecher, Henry Ward. *Yale Lectures on Preaching*. New York: Fords, Howard & Hulbert, 1893.

Bonhoeffer, Dietrich. *Life Together: Prayerbook of the Bible*. Translated by Daniel W. Bloesch and James H. Burtness. Minneapolis: Fortress, 1996.

———. *Spiritual Care*. Translated by Jay E. Rochelle. Minneapolis: Fortress, 1985.

Brooks, Phillips. *Lectures on Preaching.* London: H. R. Allenson, 1878.

Carroll, Jackson W. *As One with Authority: Reflective Leadership in Ministry.* Louisville: Westminster/John Knox, 1991.

Chrysostom, John. *On the Priesthood.* Translated by Graham Neville. Crestwood, N.Y.: St. Vladimir's Seminary Press, 1984.

―――. *On Wealth and Poverty.* Translated by Catharine P. Roth. Crestwood, N.Y.: St. Vladimir's Seminary Press, 1999.

Cozzens, Donald B., ed. *The Spirituality of the Diocesan Priest.* Collegeville, Minn.: Liturgical Press, 1997.

Craddock, Fred B. *Preaching.* Nashville: Abingdon, 1985.

Cyril of Jerusalem. *Lectures on the Christian Sacraments.* Edited by F. L. Cross. Crestwood, N.Y.: St. Vladimir's Seminary Press, 1986.

De Gruchy, John W. *Theology and Ministry in Context and Crisis: A South African Perspective.* Grand Rapids: Eerdmans, 1986.

Dittes, James E. *When the People Say No: Conflict and the Call to Ministry.* New York: Harper and Row, 1979.

Dorsey, Gary. *Congregation: The Journey Back to Church.* New York: Viking Press, 1995.

Dudley, Carl S. *Affectional and Directional Orientations to Faith.* Washington, D.C.: Alban Institute, 1982.

Dulles, Avery. *Models of the Church.* Expanded ed. New York: Doubleday, 1987.

―――. *The Priestly Office: A Theological Reflection.* New York: Paulist, 1997.

Fiddes, Paul S. *Participating in God: A Pastoral Doctrine of the Trinity.* Louisville: Westminster/John Knox, 2000.

Fox, Susan E., and Kurtis C. Hess. *Here I Am Lord: Now What? Transition and Survival in the First Parish.* South Charleston, W.Va.: Taste of Ministry, 1995.

Freedman, Samuel G. *Upon This Rock: The Miracles of a Black Church.* New York: HarperCollins, 1993.

Gregory of Nazianzus. "In Defense of His Flight to Pontus." In *The Nicene and Post-Nicene Fathers,* edited by Philip Schaff and Henry Wace, vol. 7. 2nd ser. Reprint. Grand Rapids: Eerdmans, 1983.

Gregory the Great. *Pastoral Care.* Translated by Henry Davis, S.J. New York: Newman Press, 1978.

Grierson, Denham. *Transforming a People of God.* Melbourne: Joint Board of Christian Education, 1984.

Hauerwas, Stanley. *In Good Company: The Church as Polis.* Notre Dame, Ind.: University of Notre Dame Press, 1995.

Herbert, George. *The Country Parson; The Temple.* Edited by John N. Wall, Jr. New York: Paulist, 1981.

Heschel, Abraham. *The Sabbath.* New York: Farrar, Straus and Giroux, 1951.

Hopewell, James F. *Congregation: Stories and Structures.* Edited by Barbara Wheeler. Philadelphia: Fortress, 1987.

Irenaeus of Lyons. *On the Apostolic Preaching.* Translated by John Behr. Crestwood, N.Y.: St. Vladimir's Seminary Press, 1997.

Jinkins, Michael. *Transformational Ministry: Church Leadership and the Way of the Cross.* Edinburgh: St. Andrews Press, 2002.

Jinkins, Michael, and Deborah Bradshaw Jinkins. *The Character of Leadership.* San Francisco: Jossey-Bass, 1998.

Lischer, Richard. *Open Secrets: A Spiritual Journey through a Country Church.* New York: Doubleday, 2001.

Long, Thomas G. *The Witness of Preaching.* Louisville: John Knox, 1989.

Marney, Carlyle. *Priests to Each Other.* Valley Forge, Pa.: Judson, 1974.

Mead, Loren B. *The Whole Truth about Everything Related to the Church in Twelve Pages.* Washington, D.C.: Alban Institute, 1988.

Minear, Paul S. *Images of the Church in the New Testament.* Philadelphia: Westminster, 1960.

Newbigin, Lesslie. *Foolishness to the Greeks: The Gospel and Western Culture.* Grand Rapids: Eerdmans, 1986.

Niebuhr, Reinhold. *Leaves from the Notebook of a Tamed Cynic.* New York: Harper, 1929.

Niles, D. T. *The Preacher's Task and the Stone of Stumbling.* New York: Harper and Brothers, 1958.

Oden, Thomas C. *Pastoral Theology: Essential of Ministry.* New York: Harper and Row, 1983.

Oswald, Roy M. *Crossing the Boundary between Seminary and Parish*. Washington, D.C.: Alban Institute, n.d.

———. *New Beginnings: A Pastorate Start Up Workbook*. Washington, D.C.: Alban Institute, 1989.

Peterson, Eugene H. *Five Smooth Stones for Pastoral Work*. Grand Rapids: Eerdmans, 1980.

———. *Working the Angles: The Shape of Pastoral Integrity*. Grand Rapids: Eerdmans, 1987.

Purves, Andrew. *Pastoral Theology in the Classical Tradition*. Louisville: Westminster/John Knox, 2001.

Rothauge, Arlin J. *Sizing Up a Congregation for New Member Ministry*. New York: Episcopal Church Center, n.d.

Sittler, Joseph. *Gravity and Grace: Reflections and Provocations*. Edited by Linda-Marie Delloff. Minneapolis: Augsburg, 1986.

Taylor, Barbara Brown. *The Preaching Life*. Cambridge: Cowley, 1993.

Thielicke, Helmut. *A Little Exercise for Young Theologians*. Introduction by Martin E. Marty. Grand Rapids: Eerdmans, 1962.

Thomas à Kempis. *The Imitation of Christ*. Translated by Leo Sherley-Price. London: Penguin Books, 1952.

Torrance, James B. *Worship, Community, and the Triune God of Grace*. Carlisle: Paternoster Press, 1996.

Volf, Miroslav, and Dorothy C. Bass, eds. *Practicing Theology: Beliefs and Practices in Christian Life*. Grand Rapids: Eerdmans, 2002.

Williams, Brian, and Phil Reilly. *The Potter's Rib: Mentoring for Pastoral Formation*. London: Regent College, 2004.

Willimon, William H. *Pastor: The Theology and Practice of Ordained Ministry*. Nashville: Abingdon, 2002.